The Culture of the Roman *Plebs*

The Culture of the Roman *Plebs*

Nicholas Horsfall

Bristol Classical Press

This impression 2012
First published in 2003 by
Bristol Classical Press
an imprint of
Bloomsbury Academic
Bloomsbury Publishing Plc
50 Bedford Square,
London WC1B 3DP

Copyright © 2003 by Nicholas Horsfall

All rights reserved. No part of this publication
may be reproduced, stored in a retrieval system, or
transmitted, in any form or by any means, electronic,
mechanical, photocopying, recording or otherwise,
without the prior permission of the publisher.

CIP records for this book are available from the
British Library and the Library of Congress

ISBN 978-0-7156-3238-3

Typeset by Ray Davies
Printed and bound in Great Britain by
CPI Group (UK) Ltd, Croydon, Surrey

www.bloomsburyacademic.com

Contents

Preface	7
1. Song and memory	11
2. Rules of evidence	20
3. Music returns to Rome	31
4. Culture without education; education without school	48
5. Fun for all	64
6. To help pass the time	75
7. Hypocrisy and evidence: the case of Cicero	83
8. Implications	96
Appendix 1. The legionary as his own historian	103
Appendix 2. Some inscriptions	116
Notes	129
Bibliography	167
Index	171

For AC with thanks

Preface

It all began with Petronius, whom I taught in my last year at University College London (1986-7); those classes led to a long article in 1989 which tried to keep one eye on the *Cena Trimalchionis* and the other on Richard Hoggart's *Uses of literacy*. Some positive reaction encouraged me to offer a lecture at the American Academy in Rome (May 1995) on the culture of the Roman plebs, and out of that lecture emerged both an article in the *Memoirs* of the Academy ('1996'; actually a fair while later) and a little book published in Italian at Barcelona (really 1996). Whence widespread complaints: not so much that I was wrong (allegedly I was not, by and large) but rather that the book was not conventionally on sale, nor was it in a language most British/US undergraduates would read. In the end, fun though this *samizdat* repute became, it grew clear that a more conventionally book-like book was called for and Deborah Blake very swiftly made sure it would appear with Duckworth; to her, to Susan Treggiari, Fergus Millar, Ramsay MacMullen and William Slater I am deeply grateful for this compulsion to reorganise my thoughts. Several friends and acquaintances helped me when I slipped off into periods outside the classical; Keith Thomas shared, I was delighted to find, my taste for serious cricket history.

The Culture of the Roman Plebs

By training, I am a Latinist, but Latinists always could 'do' Roman history, if they dared, just as historians have written (memorably, even) about Latin authors. Theatre and entertainment at Rome have recently attracted a lot of interest, but this book will turn out to have much more to do with the fierce current debate about the political role of the plebs than with the stage. And if it not conventionally either 'literature' or 'history', that is because I am following a particular trail wherever it leads me, under, over or round the obstacles several ancient historian friends have kindly raised in my path (see Chapters 2 and 7 in particular). Over the years I have written a good deal around the topics of this book and where I cite apparently anonymous bibliography, it is to avoid distasteful or vainglorious repetition.

I am dismayed to find how many recent books either cite the Loeb translation of ancient authors or paraphrase, when seeming to quote an actual Greek or Latin text. My translations are my own (the very few exceptions are specified), and they aim above all at reliability, which is, I hope, rarely incompatible with readability. After the first sentence of the first chapter, there is no untranslated Latin, apart from familiar or untranslatable terms. When the subject-matter is not familiar, I try to annotate heavily enough to give the reader real help with further reading.

A good deal of the thinking here first saw the light of day in talks to a sixth-form audience in a traditional and wonderfully unconventional *liceo classico* in the centre of Rome, and what I learned about non-specialist exposition there I have tried to apply here. My heartfelt thanks to Elvira Nota and to the pupils of the Liceo Visconti. Dates and mini-biographies every

Preface

time an ancient author or historical figure is mentioned are, I discovered, not the only way of reaching the non-expert reader!

John D'Arms encouraged my work on the *plebs* from its outset and I was most fortunate to be able to read a lot of his unpublished MSS; he recognised no barriers between history, literature and epigraphy, and I hope he would have enjoyed some of what follows. Robin Lane Fox's goodwill towards my line of enquiry has never been in doubt, while Ann Kuttner submitted Chapter 3 to affectionate excoriation. Numerous marginalia to *La cultura della plebs* received from Edwin Judge, Ramsay MacMullen and Nicholas Purcell are here incorporated in my argument, with thanks. Tom McGinn (Vanderbilt) and Tony Corbeill (Kansas) discussed much of this argument with me in the mid-1990s; seven years or so down the road, they were still willing to read my MS and I am profoundly grateful for their learned friendship over the years. The dedicatee cooks a grand haggis, but has contributed rather more than offal to sustain and encourage these pages.

Stanton St John, Oxon.   Nicholas Horsfall

1

Song and memory

Unum et unum duo, duo et duo quattuor: St Augustine describes this with feeling as an *odiosa cantio*, a beastly jingle.[1] 'Jingle' is the key word, for it shows that Roman children memorised their tables by chanting them (rhythmically, if not exactly tunefully) and that Roman teachers knew chanting was the best way to memorise, swiftly and simply.[2] When the teacher read out the text of Virgil, his pupils chanted back (simply, *canebamus*) the memorised verses;[3] unsurprisingly Augustine's pupil Orosius says that thereafter the text was branded, *inustum*, on the memory.[4] It was an old, widespread procedure: Cicero had called the memorisation of the Twelve Tables a *carmen*, or song, and St Jerome talks of the letters of the alphabet as a *canticum*, again best rendered 'song'.[5] Quintilian stresses the importance of memory for the orator and of beginning to train that memory from the first form;[6] the essential, realistic detail of song, though, he leaves out. The secure memorisation of sung information was even used, as we shall soon see, as an alternative to absorption via reading and writing. Tables, though, offer a warning against too neat a polarisation into oral and literate learning: leave out of it abacus and fingers; papyri (hieratic, demotic, Greek and Coptic) preserve both tables written out as school exercises and more polished, accurate versions for use as ready reckoners,[7] while Horace portrays Roman boys getting to grips with both decimal and duodecimal calculation: both division of the *as* into a hundred parts, and instant calculation of $5/12 - 1/12 = 1/3$ or $5/12 + 1/12 = 1/2$.[8] Egyptians, Greeks and Romans faced comparable problems in the absence of a simple system of numerical notation, and at Rome total familiarity with duodecimal fractions opened the gates – with one spasm of arithmetical effort – to weights and measures, the coinage and calculations of interest and of inheritance.[9]

Well-memorised tables led to well-paid work, as the paintings on Trimalchio's walls proclaimed (Petronius 29.4), celebrating how the young Trimalchio had learned accountancy (*quomodo ratiocinari didicisset*) as the foundation of a spectacular career. *Inscr. Lat. Sel.* 7753 commemorates a young man who could calculate 300 *partes*, 1/3 of 1% monthly (which was how the Romans calculated interest), i.e. 4% per annum. Back in Petronius' *Cena*, Hermeros claims proudly that he knows his capital letters and 'can recite my 1% in asses, pounds and sesterces',[10] while we've just seen that money-minded Roman boys, much to Horace's disgust, learn not poetry but percentages. Memorisation meant money, at the level of modest clerical employment. The nicer points of duodecimal fractions I leave to an appendix at the end of this chapter (pp. 17-19).

Once the memory had been awakened and put to use (and that could mean learning first nursery songs,[11] before the delights of fractions and percentages!), no surprise to discover that Romans hastened to absorb and retain more congenial material. So Ovid tells us: at the festival of Anna Perenna (the

1. Song and memory

Ides of March), when the *plebs* goes to a mass picnic on the Campus Martius: 'there they sing whatever they have learned in the theatres and to the words they nimbly clap their hands'. That *quidquid didcere theatris* has been widely recognised as a crucial scrap of information, with various implications.[12]

If the *plebs* (and that is Ovid's word; here as often, we would love to qualify and define, but our sources generally generalise, and may also exaggerate) can repeat hit songs from the theatre, they (or at least a fair number of them) must have been able to go there often enough,[13] thanks to repeated performances of the same comedy or mime, to frequent revivals of old plays (from the time of Plautus and Terence on), to *instaurationes*, repeat performances undertaken thanks to some alleged flaw in the original performance,[14] to the increase in the number of theatres available,[15] and above all, to the very sharp increase in the number of days available for *ludi* (eleven a year in Plautus' time, 101 in AD 350).[16] The simple alternative would be a crowd that could roar for one smash hit over and over again in a single performance, to learn it in one solitary sitting; an attractive idea, in itself, but a little beyond the evidence.

The *plebs* which went to the theatre often enough to memorise songs[17] also acquired necessarily an excellent knowledge of Roman theatre conventions and (most important of all) the ability to pick up unerringly any political allusion in the text, explicit or implicit.[18] This theatre public[19] was able, in AD 68,[20] with old Galba on the way to the imperial throne, to take up a line which perhaps went 'Onesimus has come from his villa' from a *notissimum canticum*, a very well-known song, from an Atellan farce; the whole audience got to the end and repeated it over and over again, with the appropriate gestures and never missing out the key words. This same public tried repeatedly to wake the tragic actor Fufius, collapsed, literally, on stage in a drunken sleep, by shouting in unison the words *mater te adpello, exsurge et sepeli me*, 'mother, I call on you, rise up and bury me'; this was a classic scene in Pacuvius' *Iliona*, but Fufius, playing Iliona herself, was not to be roused by Catienus, playing 'her' murdered son Deiphilus, not even when the whole auditorium roared the cue.[21]

With the decline of Rome, there was no decline in memorisation; indeed, rather the reverse, for the need to memorise[22] acquires an entirely new moral and spiritual profile in the hands of the Latin Fathers of the Church: with the conversion of the Roman world to Christianity, that world acquired a substantial range of texts which, in the Fathers' view, *ought* to be memorised by any serious Christian, if not simply to replace *any* non-Christian song, certainly in place of anything whatever learned in the theatre. The Creed, the Our Father, a handful of psalms and a few biblical texts were the indispensable minimum.[23] Oddly enough, though, in comparison with the Jews' urgent intensity in memorising the *Torah*,[24] and with the ancient Romans' insistence upon following the very letter of every sacred text,[25] the new religion was curiously lax (or merely realistic) when it came to memorisation. Thus, at the time of St Augustine, baptismal candidates had a week to learn the Creed. Better not to get it wrong, comments the saint, though, he adds, *we* have no stick ready to hand.[26] In Visigothic Provence, Caesarius of Arles thunders (and it is highly informative, entertaining stuff) about monks who claim to be unable to memorise psalms and biblical texts heard literally

1. Song and memory

every day.[27] Was this sheer idleness? Or aversion? Or brutish Visigothic barbarism? Caesarius is only too familiar with the excuses advanced.

Perhaps we should rather be looking at memories long used to absorbing quite different matter, often not prose, and by definition with music.[28] St Jerome[29] inveighs against priests who have laid aside Creed, Gospels and prophets so as to read comedies, to sing sexy passages of bucolic poetry (the context shows he is thinking precisely of Virgil, *Bucolics*) and to commit Virgil to memory. His illustrious contemporary St Augustine[30] provides us with a precise cultural context for Jerome's complaint, when he writes, again of Virgil, that 'few of you have known him from the text, many, from theatres';[31] that could mean, either from public readings or from dramatic performances.[32] Regular visits to the theatre, clearly, could lead to memorisation, exactly as in Ovid's day, of, for example, comic stories about maidens raped, in Lactantius' words.[33] Over three hundred years before Caesarius, Tertullian complained about husbands who sang to wives (or wives to husbands!) numbers learned from the stage or in the pub.[34] and there will be more to say about the musical life of Roman taverns (p. 31). But it is theatres that are the Latin fathers' prime targets:[35] bishops and priests[36] teach their sons (in Christ, clearly!) the reading of comedies and the low texts of mimes. Work is almost worse, when the hands are busy and the mind essentially idle: monks[37] *ought*, when at work, to sing sacred songs, *cantica ... diuina*, uplifted as though by a divine *celeuma*, or helmsman's call to keep the rhythm (p. 44); the metaphor is widespread[38] and these monks *ought* to be keeping the rhythm of their work by means of the divine rhythm

15

of sacred texts, set to suitable music. In Palestine, according to a letter sent by Eustochium to Jerome,[39] the ploughman sings 'Alleluia', the sweating reaper the psalms, and the vintage is gathered to 'something written by King David'; and indeed it is clear that some Christians did work to Christian music,[40] but others clearly did not (cf. n. 30): over and over again, early monastic rules prescribe just what it is fit that the monks ought to sing as they work.[41]

Converts, we might think, or at least young people convinced of a vocation for the religious life, would have passed naturally to Christian music and Christian words in their new existence. Not a bit of it: the divine helmsman's call (n. 36) was in practice often silent, since Augustine continues 'do we not know how all workmen (*opifices*) give their hearts and tongues to the vanities and even to the filth (*turpitudinibus*) of theatre-plays, when their hands are set to work'.[42] That suggests there were many who not only sang theatre numbers rather than hymns, but rather than traditional work-songs too. The more we recognise the widespread habit of singing theatre-songs at work, the likelier it becomes that many of our testimonies to the use of song at work (pp. 43-5) are not so much to work-songs properly speaking as to recent stage hits sung at work. In Petronius' *Cena*, most things happen to musical accompaniment, such as nail cutting (31.4) and wine serving (31.6); no case is here offered for special manicure melodies! The bulk of the songs Petronius mentions in the course of the *Cena* will most naturally have come from mime and pantomime.[43]

The Christians thundered in vain against the low morals of the theatre, and do not seem to be winning the battle for the

1. Song and memory

hearts and minds of the workforce even by the time of Caesarius: the repeated references in his sermons suggest that the issue was still of very serious concern, perhaps even of increased moment if we recognise a decline in literacy levels in the late empire[44] with, as a result, an open conflict between Christians and Pagans for the unstocked memories of the illiterate majority.[45] In early sixth-century Provence, the issue was crucial: Caesarius tells us that *everyone*, men and women, memorises and sings the Devil's songs, vile and erotic, *carmina diabolica amatoria et turpia* (not necessarily of theatrical origin) in place of Creed, Our Father, and certain psalms and antiphons;[46] he is equally appalled by the memorisation of *carmina luxuriosa*, wanton, depraved songs, learned, naturally, in place of sacred texts and sung by Christians while they danced, *ballando*.[47] Even if we allow that Caesarius was unusually concerned with song and dance, that does not mean he travesties the situation: precisely because of this bee in his bonnet, it is Caesarius who confirms that Ovid's nexus between theatre, song and memory was at the heart of popular culture and remained of dominant importance half a millennium after Ovid.

Appendix: measures and calculations

12 *unciae* to 1 *libra*; 288 (= 2 x 12 x 12) *scripulae* to 1 *libra* or *pondus* (and the *uncia* is itself divided into 12 *semisextulae*, 144 *siliquae*) (weight).
12 *pollices* to the *pes* (length).
4 *quartarii* to a *sextarius*; 48 *sextarii* to an *amphora* (liquid measure).

Cf. R.P. Duncan-Jones, *Economy of the Roman empire*² (Cambridge 1982), 269ff..

The *as* (4 to a *sestertius*, 16 to a *denarius*) is itself divided into 12 *unciae*, and these divisions of the *as* constitute the Roman system of duodecimal fractions: *semis*, for example (half an *as*) becomes the Latin for 1/2; *triens*, 4 *unciae* = 1/3 (money).

(1) How inheritances were calculated
Cicero's friend Atticus inherited from his loan-shark uncle Q. Caecilius, *ex dodrante* = 9 *unciae* = 3/4 of the estate (Nep. *Att.* 5.2).

Caecina's wife Caesennia dies (Cic. *Caec.* 17); her husband inherits *ex deunce et semuncia* (11 and a half twelfths), the freedman Aebutius *ex duabus sextulis* (a third of a twelfth), M. Fulcinius *ex sextula* (a sixth of a twelfth). Total, an *as*, or 100%.

W. Ramsay, *Manual of Roman antiquities* (London 1851), 408f. explains these mysteries, dazzlingly.

(2) How monthly interest was assessed
Cf. T. Frank, *Economic survey of ancient Rome* (Baltimore 1933), 352; we need to realise that *centesimae*, 1% per month, was used as a parallel system.

Twelve Tables, viii.18 a maximum rate of one *uncia*, 1/12 of the principal, 8 1/3%.

Cf. Liv. 7.16.1, 7.27.3, Cic. *Fam.* 5.6.2 *ex semissibus*, a monthly rate of 1/2 an *as* per month, i.e. 1/2% per month, i.e. 6% per annum.

Caecilius would not even let kin have better than *centesimis*,

1. Song and memory

1% per month, i.e. 12% per annum (Cic. *Att.* 1.12.1; 6% is *ducentesimae*, Tac. *Ann.* 2.42), while M. Brutus' agents on Cyprus exacted *quaternis*, 4% per month, i.e. 48% p.a. (Cic. *Att.* 5.21.12).

The boy who could calculate 300 *partes* (p. 12) could just as well have been commemorated as a calculator of interest *ex triente*: parallel systems of terminology have led to some slight confusion in the discussions.

Supposing we wished to calculate the monthly interest on 3,750 *sestertii* at 8% p.a.: 8% we express as 2/3 x 12/100; x 1/12 (monthly, after all, not annual interest); x 3,750: eliminating the fractions (and this stage a trained Roman will have done in a twinkling), we get 2/300 of 3,750; answer, 25 *sestertii* monthly.

2

Rules of evidence

The rhetorical figure of *anticipatio*, bringing your adversary's likely objections out into the open and answering them before they are lodged against you, is old and well-known:[1] it still has its uses, given that my methods are often not those of the orthodox Roman historian and that the view of the Roman *plebs* here offered is hardly conventional. Here therefore I offer some thoughts on how my way of 'doing' Roman social history may surprise more conventional historians, in the context of some inherent difficulties of method that any student of Roman popular ways, attitudes, even culture must face.[2]

(i) The sources this account employs cover a very wide range, some of them unexpected in a work of Roman social history; that range, though, says something about how our understanding of Roman popular culture has been transmitted and preserved and about how it was perceived in antiquity. Ovid on memorised song at a mass picnic on the Campus Martius was my starting point (p. 12f.); such incidental detail was perfectly obvious and familiar to both poet and reader and such everyday, even trivial detail, however welcome (or familiar, or agreeable) to his original public, was no more than a

2. Rules of evidence

very attractive but formally unnecessary element used to give a particular social tone to the scene (draping togas to give shade, drinking toasts to long life, dancing, mild *ivresse publique*). We can only be thankful that the poet decided there was room to record (or to visualise) and expand as much as he did.

In a particularly splendid chapter of his remarkable book, *Studien zum Verständnis der römischen Literatur* (1924), Wilhelm Kroll discussed the Romans' *Unfähigkeit zur Beobachtung*, unreadiness to observe:[3] indeed precise observation of the daily detail of popular life you only encounter in rather special circumstances, such as when Lucretius describes a man at work, in order to offer a specific, concrete, comprehensible analogy with the invisible world of atoms,[4] or when Virgil sketches swiftly a scene from daily life as an antidote, much after the manner of Homer, to the lofty tensions of epic adventure and warfare,[5] or when Seneca describes in brilliant detail what the Italians call acoustic pollution in the streets of Rome[6] in that tradition of moralising or sermonising which emerges in Latin satire or in the prose essays of Lucian, Seneca, Epictetus and St Paul, and employs from the first closely observed details of daily life to sharpen the reader's attention.[7] There are for that matter authors – Pliny the Younger and Calpurnius Siculus come to mind[8] – who appear to have a personal appetite for recording incidental detail, the cries of itinerant milk-sellers or the disappearance of travellers on Italian roads.[9]

Trivial details of humble lives are also pawns in a long literary conflict: Homer was not shocked by pigs and puddings, though many of his critics later were.[10] However, realism gained in the end a sure foothold in Alexandrian literature. Thus elements of precise detail, rough and dour, enter Theocritus' representation of shepherds' lives and even survive into Virgil's charming pastoral poses in the *Bucolics*.[11] The author of the pseudo-Virgilian *Moretum* spends a hundred lines on the kitchen preparations of a market-gardener and his (?) slave companion: startlingly, much of what we learn from this singular text about lighting hearths from the embers and wearing goatskins and leggings we already knew from earlier texts.[12] But the life of the *urban* poor is less attractive to the Roman author than that of ploughmen or shepherds and it is almost miraculous that we know as much as we do about life in a Roman *insula*, or tenement block;[13] we depend for our knowledge upon a vast mass of discontinuous detail, literary and archaeological, detail preserved for the most varied reasons, and not from any sense of the *insula*-dweller's right to literary immortality. Behind Lindsey Davis (whose detail is generally admirable and almost too full at times!), there crowd the handbooks of, for example, Friedlaender, Marquardt, Blümner, Paoli, Carcopino, Becker, Balsdon. Their footnotes (not exhaustive or comprehensive) reflect a vast miscellaneous accumulation of varied trivia. Pure chance has thrust into our hands a really imposing bulk of such scattered information, as I discovered, for example, when first exploring the cries of Roman street-vendors, or subsequently, the fragments of Roman work-songs.[14] Detail — or silence: what did the workman in the Roman street wear under his tunic? Or on his head? You might have suspected that we knew, but we do not.[15]

There is a precise point to this circuitous line of thought: our evidence is often patchy and preserved by wild chance; we need therefore to be alert in our use of arguments from silence.

2. Rules of evidence

Take popular songs of contemporary content (not triumph-songs, not acclamations), such as are recorded about, for example, Sulla and Germanicus.[16] Suetonius is rather interested by such texts, but Cicero does not mention them even in his letters, for all his frequent attention to public opinion as expressed by the theatre crowd (p. 39ff.). So, in this case, it looks as though Cicero preferred to ignore such epigrams and songs because they really were of no particular political or human interest in his (do we call it prejudiced, or limited?) view of the matter. If, then, we turn back to memorisation, Ovid gives us the vital clue, and we find a scatter of hints that memorisation never ceased to matter in the Roman world; for the rest, silence, because memorisation is so obvious, banal, routine, until we reach authors to whom the use of the memory and the sort of songs memorised have become fundamentally important issues of pastoral discipline. Equally, Provence's theatrical culture was conventionally Roman and there are no regional variations in the Fathers' criticisms of pagan theatre, so the thousand kilometres between Ovid and Caesarius may matter as little as the five hundred years. In other words, the transmission of the evidence here used may not in the end be quite as skewed by chance and distance as might at first sight appear.

(ii) That may seem rather too brisk a dismissal of the risk of chronological and geographical distortion of the evidence. The historian of the arena can trace some development and variation[17] in the programme of beast-fights and gladiatorial combats offered, and there is likewise, as might have been predicted, some change in the circus too.[18] But continuity dominates in the Christian attacks[19] upon popular culture, whether in Greek or Latin, and whether the target is theatre, amphitheatre or circus; in part, Christian rhetoric against gladiatorial combats indeed draws on the Stoics; much more important, the targets themselves change so very little, from Augustus to Justinian, from the Euphrates to the Tagus; contrast the continuous, even headlong change observed by recent historians of cricket, a sport many would judge (wrongly!) to be a symbol of traditionalist immutability.[20] It is no surprise to discover that Christian hymns owe a very great deal to their pagan predecessors (certainly in content, possibly in music),[21] that between the first rhythmical acclamations in Julius Caesar's time and Byzantine court usage there is unbroken continuity,[22] and that very possibly there is an uninterrupted line of descent between the triumph-songs of the Roman republic and Byzantine political song.[23] We may therefore return a little more reassured to the proposition that behind Caesarius' preaching there lay a long tradition of memorised popular song: a decline in literacy may, we saw, have brought oral, memorised culture back into prominence (p. 16f.), but when, three hundred years earlier, Tertullian complained about married life corrupted by unChristian warblings in the home (p. 15), the Roman world was at least as literate as when Ovid had written of the Campus Martius echoing to theatre choruses.

A good song fires and draws our memories; its original content, context and character are, relatively, of secondary importance. The survival of non-Christian song (much of it from the theatre) in the late empire remains a bulwark of cheerfully impenitent paganism;[24] that was where its roots lay.

2. Rules of evidence

I would suppose that it was more cheerful, more entertaining, more *fun*, just *better*, though in the end the Church would raid the repertoire of popular song in the interest of winning back the ears and memories of the faithful.[25] The chronological links in this argument are not as solid as those in a discussion of Caesar's policies in 49 BC, but in the end they may for all that come to seem less outrageous, not least if analogies can be offered in passing to comparable phenomena from other ancient or modern cultures.

Part of the objection was always to a way of looking at the Romans (more musical, more oral in their culture) that is gradually becoming less unfamiliar. Rosalind Thomas has brought oral culture firmly back to its proper place in the life of classical Athens;[26] for Rome, there has been an increasing amount of speculation about oral and performance elements latent in our literary texts,[27] some rather feverish and ultimately unconvincing controversy about oral transmission and the 'facts' of early Roman history,[28] and some useful restatement of evidence long known to specialists on oral elements in Roman legal procedures.[29] Nor indeed were the Romans necessarily, by dispensation of Jupiter and by order of the Twelve Tables, tone-deaf. A proper understanding of their musicality is creeping back into our awareness;[30] it will take longer for certain deep prejudices about their culpable un-Greekness to die. Given how widely attested and generally familiar music-oriented, memory-based oral cultures are among the anthropologists and historians of popular culture,[31] the very notion that another such oral culture might have coexisted at Rome with the stiffer but more familiar world of

The Culture of the Roman Plebs

Virgil, Tacitus and their readers becomes perhaps a little less startling.

(iii) My use of *'plebs'* or of 'popular culture' may at first sight seem unnerving or irresponsible to the conventional Roman historian, but it should not be supposed that I write without awareness of the issue.

By comparison with – let us say – studies of priests of the imperial cult at Puteoli under Vitellius – it may seem magniloquent and irresponsible to talk amply about 'the Roman *plebs*' and it is fair to ask for a rather more precise definition of what I am talking about. Fair, but not altogether realistic. In his introduction to the now 'classic' *Plebs and Princeps*, Zvi Yavetz[32] recognises that this problem has several dimensions;[33] it is more than clear that the tangle of definitions is *not* going to be sorted out and the systematic application of precise terminology is best abandoned. Let me offer a very swift sketch-map of the tangled definitions:

(1) The terms *populus, plebs, turba* (perhaps the word nearest to 'mob'), *multitudo, vulgus* (to which a contemptuous adjective is often added) may be interchangeable but cannot be assumed to be so; *plebs Romana* and *populus Romanus* are far from synonymous.[34]

(2) So too 'the whole crowd', the whole theatre', 'the populace', 'all those present', 'the *plebs*' are familiar generalisations, or exaggerations, in ancient authors,[35] not the outcome of precisely conducted surveys.

(3) You could not determine the status of a Roman by where (s)he lived; too many exceptions to the 'pattern' existed.[36]

(4) You could not always determine status by accent or

2. Rules of evidence

dress;[37] the toga covered a multitude of status-differences, and we do not forget that Ovid's March picnic crowd draped their togas to improvise awnings. Senators naturally wore them too![38] But there was no guarantee that a senator spoke passable Latin.[39]

(5) Elevated rank was no guarantee of superior education.[40]

(6) Contempt for the man who earned money (worse if he did so by his own hands) was a widely held socio-literary posture, not the article of a creed and far from universally binding. Even those arch-snobs, our surviving Latin authors, admit occasionally that not all lucre is equally filthy.[41]

(7) 400,000 sesterces made you a knight; 394,000 was not enough. Many very prosperous Romans were not knights.[42]

(8) Within the *populus Romanus*, there were vast distinctions of wealth, standing and permissible activity in public life.[43]

(9) Political involvement was likely to be determined by your address, or your work, or your income, or your town of origin, or your patron, or your kin, or your friends, or more probably by some combination of the above. No two Roman citizens were likely to be subject to exactly the same sets of pressures.[44]

(10) Monday's rioter was Tuesday's voter. Tuesday's voter was Thursday's theatregoer. Not necessarily with the same friends and loyalties in each context.[45]

(11) Almost any piece of evidence used in my argument is therefore open to disqualification on one ground or another and many of the same objections will be applicable to a lot of modern Roman social history. Do I offer a bigger, brighter, better house of cards? Or does concentration upon attitudes

and states of mind save a writer from some of the dangers of method and obstacles to generalisation which threaten many more orthodox studies of the Roman *plebs*?

In this book, I present a lot of sometimes unfamiliar evidence: what it says is more important than what I say and I only hope I do not misrepresent the man in the Roman street or what in passing ancient authors wrote about him. I try to use their terminology, not my own, and any resulting disorder is therefore largely ancient, not modern. Who is the plebeian I am writing about? Perhaps above all, and even before M. Didius Falco, Volteius Mena, the used-goods dealer whom we know from Horace's seventh *Epistle*;[46] for the rest, I label them as I find them in the authors: they are largely free (freed, too, in some contexts) but sub-equestrian in status, and Latin-speaking; if the evidence permitted, more of them would be female.

(iv) There remains the very bad press that the Roman *plebs* often enjoyed in antiquity. Thus, the argument seems to go, if Juvenal can write of Remus' mob, the *turba Remi* (10.81) which longs for just two things, bread, naturally, and circuses, *panem et circenses*, then who are we to explore their intellects and culture?[47] Such inferences are hasty and imprudent, not least because behind Juvenal there stretches an interesting ancestry: it was long ago noted[48] that for Cleopatra the issue (or denial) of corn at Alexandria was of prime importance[49] and a circus (or rather hippodrome) had been built by the first Ptolemy.[50] In Juvenal's day, Dio Chrysostom reports an old saying that the populace (*plethos*) of Alexandria cared for nothing else if they had good store of bread and a show of horses[51] and before that Aristophanes had jibed at the Atheni-

2. Rules of evidence

ans' concern for their bellies and eagerness to make all they could get out of their *polis*.[52] Actually Juvenal's accusations are so familiar and apparently weighty because they are so memorably formulated, but their specific content had been going the rounds for a good while.[53] I don't want to suggest that the high-minded Roman plebeian was happy to do without a full belly and a day at the races. Not at all. But the mind-set that makes of the loaf on your plate at home, and that other loaf beside the home straight two grave accusations is already familiar enough from our scraps of Greek oligarchic writing,[54] while Juvenal's barb belongs also to a rich collection of insults at the *plebs*' expense, to be collected from across the whole range of Latin literary texts.[55] Was the Roman populace 'scoundrel dregs' simply because it was said to be, often enough?[56] Hardly! The language of Latin rhetoric and courtroom polemic was indeed very highly coloured[57] and here draws upon a rhetoric, and lexicon, of patrician contempt which lay open for any orator to draw upon. Cicero, after all, can flatter the ear and wits of his popular hearers in one speech, and in another, before an élite audience, lash that same populace with insult.[58] Inasmuch as Juvenal wrote of popular enthusiasm for free bread and the races, there was also a solid element of accuracy in the observation (cf. n. 53). Columella, a technical, specialist agricultural writer, looses off at the city slave population 'an idle and sleepy race, used to leisure, the Park, the circus, theatres, dicing, bars, brothels'.[59] A rich recipe for an undemanding, happy and varied life, we might try to protest. Or let us concede to Columella a touch of dyspeptic accuracy, alongside a fine choice of vices already familiar from the range of charges Roman orators habitually flung at their opponents,[60] a well-stocked supermarket shelf of ready-use slanders, behind which the specialist notices old oppositions of country/city, honest ploughboy/city slicker, virtue/vice, austerity/luxury, a nexus of oppositions indeed which it is easy to trace back from Horace, Virgil and Livy via the pages of Varro, and the way in which Gaius Marius and the elder Cato presented themselves, to Greece, to Xenophon in particular, and to Hesiod, perhaps a contemporary of Homer's.[61]

The Romans' passion for gaming is undoubted historical fact,[62] but just as objectively real is the traditional and rhetorical manner in which gaming and comparable pastimes or entertainments were presented. Whether pleasant relaxations or corrupting vices, they coexisted alongside a wide range of rather more clearly 'cultural' (or at least, demanding) interests, which are overdue for revaluation (Chapters 5, 6, 7). But what these pages have been careful not to mention is literacy (cf. p. 72ff.), or at least the distinct abilities to read, write and count, abilities which depended frequently (generally, even) not upon school, but upon alternative methods (in the home, at work, in the army, etc.);[63] we have already considered the possibility that (many) accountants made do with ready-reckoners and memorised tables of fractions (p. 11f.), and in the following chapters it will become clearer still that literacy is not essential to the whole range of those social or cultural pastimes dear to a Roman plebeian which required some degree of intellectual engagement. These pastimes, moreover, were themselves, it turns out, in some sense educative; life in the Subura was not a haze (not *just* a haze, perhaps) of sour wine, diceboxes and cast-aside garments.

3

Music returns to Rome

It has now begun to emerge that the Romans did in fact have an active oral culture, and one that was rooted in the trained memory. It is therefore also high time to recall that as a people they were intensely musical.[1] The Romans sang, often and most willingly, as part of a wide, much-relished musical heritage, and thereafter remembered what they had heard sung, and so we should look rather more closely at that Roman musical culture, as expressed in instrumental music, dance and song.[2] It is no great surprise that players are attested at both ends of the social scale: at one end, the Syrian girl, chief attraction and perhaps also owner of the tavern in the short poem *Copa*;[3] she plays pipe, flute, castanets, syrinx (?) and strings, and neither her easy morals nor her music are at all out of place in a Roman tavern.[4] At the other end of the scale, there is Sallust's famous portrait of the noble Sempronia, who was trained *psallere saltare elegantius quam necesse est probae*, to play and to dance more stylishly than a good woman should.[5] About 430 AD, Macrobius commented acutely on Sallust's sketch: best if she had not learned at all – for musical education there was, for both sexes[6] – but, given that she had obstinately persisted in learning, she should at least have been bad enough not to give pleasure. The point was that skill inevitably made men think of the talents expected of a salaried professional, of humble rank, or of a whore, who played in the exercise of her own profession.[7] The real expert, almost worse, became a symbol of the new, imported, luxurious arts of Greece, for that is how they appeared to the noisily and determinedly prejudiced. Of course, by the late republic, the professional personnel and terminology of music as entertainment at Rome, like much of the technical development of the art itself, was indeed Greek,[8] and 'this modern music' could be represented as shocking/depraved, not only in its moral ethos,[9] but in the immorality of many of its performers (above, n. 7), so it may need to be spelled out once and for all: what we think of as traditional Roman prejudice ('new is worse', 'development is degeneration', etc.); has no bearing on the content and attitudes of popular culture,[10] and I detect no points at which 'traditional Roman values' actually affect that popular culture in general or the growth of music in particular.

Above all, music in the world of Trimalchio, as represented by Petronius, has been startlingly neglected and we are still waiting for a detailed analysis of the abundant material.[11] There was nothing implausible in portraying Trimalchio, a vastly rich freedman of (?)Syrian origin, as passionately devoted to music: that passion orchestrated both the composition of his household in general and, more specifically, the evening of the *Cena*. So there was to Petronius nothing incompatible between a passion for music so widespread as to be a clearly major element in the detailed characterisation of Trimalchio and his eastern origins, years of slavery in Italy, huge success in trade as a freedman, and illimitably vulgar tastes. In fact, Petronius enlarges or exaggerates a well-attested

3. Music returns to Rome

Roman passion for *Tafelmusik*:[12] it could be wondrously respectable, as when the elder Cato (*Origines* frag. 118 Peter) writes of the 'habit' of singing the praises of famous men at banquets, a practice widely attested from ancient Persia to Anglo-Saxon Britain which is unfortunately quite likely to have reached Cato from his reading of Dicaearchus and not from observation or a reliable source,[13] or, quite as often, not respectable at all.[14] It is intensely frustrating that amid the great mass of information we have on the Roman *collegia*, clubs or associations of employees, craftsmen, and workmen, who met for solidarity, society, charity, or worship, we know virtually nothing about their banquets (or at least, communal meals) and the entertainments held at their end, and very little of the food; that little seems improbably austere (bread and sardines, *Inscr. Lat. Sel.* 7212.2.15, and that really seems to be all that we know, red herrings aside). The regulations on good behaviour are detailed enough to suggest that some perceptible quantity of wine was served,[15] but there is not a word on the entertainment. That is not to say there was none, which would have been out of keeping with everything we know about the Roman social evening. The silence therefore is not significant, dearly though we would love to know how the pork-butchers and bricklayers of Puteoli celebrated.

Such love of instrumental music prevailed in the Roman world that even animals followed their owners' tastes: thus pigs were trained to do everything to the sound of the horn they knew and loved,[16] and we learn that the use of instrumental music (for a human audience) spread to priests (or their assistants), shepherds, soldiers and waiters.[17]

Waiters, goats (n.16), and consulars, even emperors: musical ability or disposition becomes an element deserving of biographical or anecdotal record, from the age of L. Licinius Crassus (consul 95 BC: his friend Numerius Furius sang when he felt like it; as a boy *didicit quod discendum*, he learned what was necessary, Cic. *De orat.* 3.87) on, via Sempronia, the trumpet-playing consul Norbanus (AD 19; Dio 57.18.3f.) down to Nero, Titus, Marcus Aurelius and Commodus.[18] Whether that meant that a shoemaker might quite normally and unexceptionally play the flute in his spare time I do not think we know; certainly, nothing suggests that an amateur plebeian flautist would have been in any way odd.

At Maecenas' house, music[19] was played to put him to sleep, 'when distressed about his personal life and grieved for the daily snubs of his grumpy wife, Terentia'. More to the point, when Augustus wanted music at dinner, he summoned not his own *symphoniaci*, but a group belonging to Toronius Gallus, a *mango*, or slave-dealer, one of the most despised occupations in all the Roman social hierarchy;[20] this chart-topping band, apparently Toronius Gallus' own, rather than a group he was in the course of selling, was not, however, always available, for their owner did once reply 'they're working at the millstones',[21] as slaves undergoing punishment. That suggests there was no sharp distinction between court and popular music or a least that there was no solid front of aristocratic disdain for the musical entertainments of lesser men; we shall indeed find time and again that in practice the social division of taste that one might expect on the basis of familiar literary sources simply did not exist.

Dance is accepted with the same widespread enthusiasm as instrumental music, and encounters a very similar kind of

3. Music returns to Rome

moral hesitation in the texts: we have seen that Sempronia was too good for a lady of her rank (p. 31f.). And a woman who danced well risked aligning herself beside the boozy Levantine bar-girl of *Copa*, who *saltat lasciva* (v. 3), dances lewdly.[22] Trimalchio's wife too still danced with gusto, and seems (though the text is briefly corrupt at the crucial point, *Sat.* 52.11) to have begun life as a dancer. Romans had long preferred to assume that dancers were necessarily persons of deplorable morals: Macrobius explains that between 204 and 149 even the children of senators regularly went to dance-schools (3.14.4), and competed in their skill (*certatim*) but the first thunders of specific protest that he quotes are not from the elder Cato (see p. 36 below) but from Scipio Aemilianus, in his speech on the *Lex iudiciaria* of Tib. Gracchus, 129 BC; the objection was chiefly to free-born children of tender years associating with their low, lewd actor teachers and learning steps that even some shameless slave could not decently execute.[23] In the late republic, it is clear, though, that senators and their wives danced with enthusiasm and that Cicero's expressions of outrage were not enough to stop them.[24] Usage had far outrun protest, though the younger Pliny continues dutifully to complain.[25] In Visigothic Provence, nothing had changed: Bishop Caesarius' flock[26] danced on church festivals,[27] their pastor thundered, and his successors would continue to do so, in vain, for dancing at Christian festivals persisted into the twentieth century;[28] and when, at Barcelona as late as 1996, I tentatively asked Prof. José O'Callaghan, SJ about the survival of ritual dance among Christians of the Mozarabic rite (centered on Toledo), he smiled cheerfully and nodded in assent! Several other instances will emerge of the remarkable durability of ancient popular usage[29] and of its unfailing ability to rise above moralising protest.

Lastly, song. We have again to strip our evidence of some misleading or alarming moral and conceptual incrustations: early or simple song (so too dance, instrumental music) is damned as rough or rustic, while sophisticated developments are, naturally 'over-refined' or even 'degenerate'; this apparently serious criticism has distracted too many students of ancient Rome from the central fact of the delight the ancient Romans, at all levels, took in song.[30] Romans of good family aroused surprise, even criticism, but sang nevertheless: thus the elder Cato protested at the tribune (?) M. Caelius singing when he felt like it (*Orat.* frag. 115) at which Macrobius is surprised, for he knows that many old Romans thought song really quite respectable (*Sat.* 3.14.10 *non inter turpia numeratum*). And distinguished Romans are indeed attested as singing, even well, like Sulla (Macr. 3.14.10), Numerius Furius and Sempronia (pp. 31, 34). Traditionalist censure clearly did not stop either the crowds on 15 March (p. 12f.), or the many songsters of mixed ability in Trimalchio's household,[31] or, five hundred years later, Caesarius of Arles' disobedient flock (p. 14f.). For it was not only in late antiquity that Romans sang as they worked; that they had always done, no less than the Greeks.[32] At Rome, to be sure, much of what was sung at work was not, properly speaking, work-songs, but rather, so far as we can judge (p. 16), words and tunes from the theatre. Gladiators, travellers, waiters, lovers, diners, soldiers, boatmen and demonstrators all sang (see Appendix A at the end of this chapter for the evidence, where some of the occasions on which song was particularly familiar are also collected). I add

3. Music returns to Rome

as Appendix B to this chapter the few fragments we have of Roman popular song, of various types, to confirm the impression that only the tiny top of a vast missing iceberg survives.

In the *Digest*, Ulpian (round AD 200) observes (in the context of what constitutes actionable *infamia*, public ill-repute) 'if someone writes a song or puts it up, or sings something which harms someone's decency'.[33] That suggests that in some cases posted broadsheet song (quite possibly, old tune, new words, as in the case of – e.g. – *Beggar's Opera*, or *Fred Karno's Army*) could catch on to good effect. Aulus Gellius refers (*Noct. Att.* 4.5.5) to a *versus scite factus cantatusque esse a pueris urbe tota fertur*, 'it was said that a witty line was composed and sung by boys all over the city'. The verse was old and proverbial ' bad advice is worst of all to the giver':[34] all Gellius does is offer a pretty, circumstantial fantasy to account for the popular verse *malum consilium consultori pessimum est*, in fact a rendering of Hesiod, *Works and days* 266: the words, then, are not necessarily old or popular in origin, but whatever the text is, and however weak the explanation of its origin is, by modern criteria, there is no reason why Gellius should have dressed his account up with details palpably silly or implausible.[35]

The crowd in the ancient Roman street was evidently not particularly meek, taciturn and orderly (of quiet let us not speak, even);[36] song, sometimes contemporary, political, topical and irreverent, if not grossly abusive, was a strong element in that tornado of noise which reached up menacingly from – to speak approximately and provocatively – Subura to Palatine.[37] Not, though, a mere confused racket, for popular song and chant were strongly rhythmic, and that is a classic aid to memorisation;[38] the scurrilous songs traditionally sung at triumphs for evidently apotropaic reasons were apparently always in one and the same hammering rhythm (cf. p. 65 for a form of the trochaic tetrameter as the quintessential popular verse), the same indeed as the hymn 'tántum érgo sácraméntum', or for that matter as Robert Browning's 'Nobly, nobly Cape St Vincent to the North-West died away'. Perhaps because they lack the thematic unity, the historic significance and the simple fun of the *versus triumphales* (see below, pp. 65, 111f.), the outbursts of joy and relief which are attested in exactly the same metre and were thus presumably sung, as the triumph-songs explicitly were,[39] have never attracted the same degree of attention. So Tiberius was woken by the voices of a crowd[40] congratulating him and singing on all sides *salva Roma, salva patria, salvus est Germanicus*, 'Rome is saved, the nation is saved, Germanicus is saved'. We really know nothing of the composition or authorship of such songs[41] but shall soon see that a good deal of fairly safe speculation is possible on how they were launched and distributed; even before the day of the cyclostyled flysheet, the composition and organisation of apparently spontaneous and politically significant songs of praise (or the reverse!) or of a few lethal and easily memorable couplets written up legibly at a few strategic points around the city was, as I now try to show, relatively simple.[42]

To conclude this chapter, we must look more specifically at the issue of control: if the suggestion that memorised song or chant really was an instrument of politics finds acceptance, and even more so if such songs and chants are promoted to a provisional role as a key (one of several) to understanding the hearts and minds of the Roman plebs, then we need to ask

3. Music returns to Rome

more specifically whether we have any idea of how such material could be learned, controlled, even manipulated.

In the *Pro Sestio* (56 BC), Cicero discusses (§115) displays of public opinion (assemblies, elections, and, most important, the theatre), during his exile, the previous year: 'let me turn to the games .... Demonstrations of opinion (*significationes*) are sometimes straight (*verae*), sometimes flawed and corrupt. They say that theatrical and gladiatorial assemblies (*consessus*) tend usually to raise a light and scattered applause, bought through the irresponsibility of a few men (*levitate non nullorum emptos plausus*)'. When that happens, continues Cicero, you can tell how and through whom it happens. And never do you get wrong the sound of real applause raised by the bulk of the citizen body.[43]

No surprise that if you could buy an election, or a riot, or the passing of a bill, or a verdict, you could also buy, or try to buy, an audience. The younger Pliny complains that the public in the centumviral court are *conducti et redempti*, hired and bought (*Epist.* 2.14.4): terms are reached with a *manceps*, contractor, and the cash is handed over in open court. Twelve sesterces a time (§6), and there were those who made a living of sorts by hiring their lungs to trial after trial! Theatre and stadium offered the chance of manipulation on a far larger scale: bits of the transaction can sporadically be glimpsed, and the rest reconstructed with fair confidence. The would-be purchaser treated with the likes of Percennius the mutineer, whom Tacitus called *dux olim theatralium operarum*, 'once leader of a theatre claque',[44] well-trained (*doctus*) in throwing into confusion (*miscere*) the public (*coetus*) through his support of actors (*theatrali studio*): this was a role once actually adopted by Nero, 'simultaneously the leader (*signifer*) and spectator of unrest among the pantomimes' (Suet. *Nero* 26.2). *Domini*, leaders of the *factiones* (Suet. *Nero* 5.2, 22.2), are usually thought of as businessmen who hired out the necessary equipment for putting on a day's racing,[45] and they received the generous sum of 400,000 sesterces a year under Nero (Suet. *Nero* 20.3). But the faction heads (*capita*) of Suetonius *Tiberius* 37.3 (for which *domini*, chiefs, does look like an obvious and natural synonym) are clearly leaders of theatre claques too and we need to remember that claques were active in theatre, arena and circus alike,[46] backing respectively actors, weapons and, at least under the early empire, teams, or stables, if not colours. Shouts of approval which did not respect the rhythm[47] were almost as bad as a break, or actual silence, or as applause on the wrong occasion (Suet. *Galba* 6.2; cf. Epict. 3.4). There were times when soldiers, probably praetorians (Tac. *Ann.* 1.77.1, 13.24.1) were stationed between the blocks of seats, to touch up the public's backs in the theatre and make sure that orders were respected.[48] Gentler methods were appropriate in the centumviral court: rousing cheers when the chorusmaster (*mesochorus*) signalled (Pliny *Epist.* 2.14.6). For applause, at least from the reign of Nero, was a fine art, or so at least was the *plausus compositus*, 'regulated applause', with its *certi modi*, 'regular cadences'.[49] Nero was enchanted by the rhythmic shouts of approval of some recent immigrants to Naples and summoned others from Egypt. Young equestrians and a good five thousand stoutly built young plebeians[50] were divided into squads and were trained as 'cheer-leaders', each for a particular type of applause, the booms, *bombi*, the tiles, *imbrices* and the curved tiles, *testas*![51]

3. Music returns to Rome

But hard cash and the big stick are not quite the end of the matter, as recent work on the organisation of seating in the Roman theatre and the extraordinary new inscriptional material from Aphrodisias suggest: seating certainly could be and very possibly often, even always, was assigned via associations (*collegia*) local, trade, and religious.[52] So if you learned the required songs[53] or chants or applause with your neighbourhood friends, or with your fellow-bakers, or with other frequenters of the cult of Serapis, they did not have to be learned in risky haste on the day. But this is not to say we have discovered the mechanisms of an efficient system of manipulated diffusion: the frequent disorders in the theatre, a venue far less stable and orderly than the arena and one which was never effectively controlled,[54] along with a deep-rooted tradition of theatrical protest by allusion, allusion that was joyously spotted and applauded by an expert public,[55] suggest that efficient control was no more than a dream to the authorities, one that remains to delude historians committed to a view of the plebs as systematically managed and exploited by some form of state or aristocratic apparatus. Better yet, if we have identified something of how songs and chants were 'launched' from above, we have also, necessarily, identified[56] a system equally well suited to the memorisation and diffusion of disrespect, abuse and protest, a rich and unexhausted popular voice, as Tacitus and Suetonius well knew.[57] Thus when we read of some satiric epigram[58] or disrespectful *carmen*[59] as 'spread about', *vulgatum* (and many comparable expressions are quoted in this chapter), the pleasant suspicion grows that this was done sometimes at least through the very system (either way round, partly improvised, flexible, informal, and therefore peculiarly supple, durable and potent) devised for the public expression of approval, adulation and applause. Caesar had complained of the *uersiculis de Mamurra perpetua stigmata imposita*, the indelible brands laid upon him by the epigrams upon Mamurra (Suet. *Caes.* 73.1): scribbled up (let us remember Ulpian's view of graffiti, p. 37), shouted out over a drink in the *schola* (club-house) of a *collegium*, chanted in the street, even sung; we are left with a positive excess of possible methods for embarrassing diffusion (cf. p. 23 for Cicero's silence on political songs).

Just as the study of Byzantine circus factions begins with the theatre riots of the early principate (Cameron, n. 43) and just as the origins of Byzantine chant can be traced back to Roman republican crowds (above, p. 24), so the role of organised song and chant can be confirmed and further illustrated by what happens in the early church[60] when hymns, rather than 'songs'[61] are used to spread the dangerous doctrines of heresy and schism, by (for example) Gnostics, Marcionites, Arians, Priscillianists and Donatists, and likewise for the reply of orthodox belief, by Irenaeus, Methodius and above all Augustine, who writes (*Retractationes* 1.20, *Patr. Lat.* 32.617) about his *Psalmus contra partem Donati*, Psalm against Donatus' cause, 'I wanted the Donatist cause to reach the knowledge of the very humblest folk, of the inexpert, of the simple, and, so far as we could, to stick in their memory'.[62] He therefore composed a psalm with a chorus for all to use, in verses with initial letters in alphabetic sequence to help memorisation. I doubt whether Sulla, himself a singer of distinction, will have been exactly clumsy or inexpert in handling essentially the same instrument of diffusion.

3. Music returns to Rome

Appendix A: songs in their social context

(1) Songs at triumphs: cf. pp. 65, 111f.

(2) Songs at weddings: *Fescennini versus, qui canebantur in nuptiis*, Paul. exc. Fest. p. 76.6, Horsfall, *Riv. Fil.* 122 (1994), 65.

(3) Political songs and chants: cf. p. 23 above.

(4) It is possible that the cries of street-vendors – which I collect at *Invigilata Lucernis* 13-14 (1991-2), 173, after (e.g.) H.J. Loane, *Industry and commerce of the city of Rome* (Baltimore 1938), 149, MacMullen (1974), 169, n. 20 – on occasion passed over into actual song, but that is not guaranteed by Sen. *Ep.* 56.3 *insignita modulatione vendentes*, 'selling with a distinctive modulation'. Whether shepherds really sold milk at the crossroads *cantu pastorali*, with pastoral song, Philarg. *ad* Virg. *Buc.* 3.26 – is not quite clear: cf. my discussion at *Class. Rev.* 43 (1993), 269.

(5) Songs used by mothers and nurses, Persius 3.16ff., with scholiasts, Wille, 149. Note p. 81 for nurse-culture.

(6) Songs to relax at bedtime: cf. Quint. 9.4.12, Wille, 147-9, and n. 19 above.

(7) Soldiers' songs: rather a mystery (see n. 17); imitated from the Germans, according to Wille, 138. See Ammianus Marcellinus 22.4.6, 31.7.11. It bears repetition (cf. Horsfall cited n. 17) that the Roman army can hardly have marched to victory from Cadiz to Caucasus without song. See below, p. 139.

(8) Music at mealtimes: cf. (for example) Cic. *Verr.* 2.3.105, 5.92, *Pro Gallio* frag. 1, Sen. *Dial.* 7.11.4, and in general, n. 12. Note also n. 21 (Augustus), n. 11 (Trimalchio) and p. 97f. (*carmina convivalia*).

(9) Sailors and boatmen: cf. Wille, 123 and above p. 15 for the *celeuma*; the steersman's call was rhythmic but not strictly musical. Passages such as Ovid *Trist.* 4.1.10 (*in numerum*), Quint. 1.10.16 (*cantus*), Mart. 3.67.3 (*celeuma*) do not, despite Wille, 122-4, refer necessarily to music at the helm and a hammer, the *portisculus*, was in fact used to give the beat. But note oarsmen's songs: Rutil. Namat. 1.370, Sid. Apoll. *Epist.* 2.10, v. 27ff. (cf. Chapter 1, p. 15) and perhaps *Paneg. Lat.* 10 (Mamert.) 12.7.

(10) Beggars: our texts are likely to refer to chants, rather than actual songs; see Horace, *Epist.* 1.17.48 (with Porphyrio's note), Persius 1.88ff. with scholiasts.

(11) Lovers: as St Augustine remarks, *cantare amantis est*, 'song is typical of a lover' (*Serm.* 336.1 = *Patrol. Lat.* 38.1472). Cf. Sen. *Epist.* 51.12, Hor. *Carm.* 3.7.29-32, *Serm.* 1.5.15, the drunken boatman who sings of his *absentem ... amicam*, absent girlfriend, Caesarius *Serm.* 6.3 *cantica diabolica amatoria et turpia*, 'the devil's songs, erotic, and low'.

(12) Travellers: Hor. *Serm.* 1.5.15ff. (above), 1.7.30f., Juvenal 10.22 *cantabit vacuus coram latrone viator*, the man who travels light will sing before the bandit, Ausonius, *Mosella* 165ff., the traveller and the boatman (167) *probra canunt seris cultoribus*, sing out insults to those late at work in the fields.

(13) Shepherds: cf. n. 16 and §4 above, Prop. 4.10.27-30. Our evidence for shepherds' songs proper is almost hopelessly confused by the association with pastoral poetry. Ennodius' preface to his *Carm.* 1.8 (ed. Vogel, pp. 29f.) may be an exception. It is of course *prima facie* likely that they did sing! Their songs at rustic festivals (Tib. 2.5.87f.; cf. 1.7.39-44, 2.1.51-6, Ovid *Am.* 3.10.47f., Hor. *Carm.* 3.18.15f., Verg. *G.*

3. Music returns to Rome

1.349f., 2.385f., 417) are equally credible, but not demonstrably 'authentic' since the sources are again 'polluted' by Greek literary accounts of rustic festivities: see my discussion, cited at §2, 67.

(14) Work-songs: cf. Wille, 107-10. Note, for example, songs at the loom, (Verg. *G.* 1.293, with my note on *Aen.* 7.12), in the laundry (Titinius *com.* frag. 28; O. Ribbeck, *Com. Rom. Frag.*² (Leipzig 1873), 137), on the chaingang, digging the fields (Tib. 2.6.26, Ovid *Trist.* 4.1.5f.), grinding grain (*Moretum* 29f.), gathering the vintage (Tib. 1.7.35f., Varro *Sat. Men.* 363). For Christian work-song, cf. p. 15f.

Appendix B: fragments of songs

Cf. G.B. Pighi, *Lyra Romana* (Milano 1946), 67-147, K. Büchner, *Fragmenta poetarum Latinorum* (Leipzig 1982), 41-3: each collects much of the same material. See too Courtney (1993), 470-82. I exclude spells and songs of a religious character and do not aim at an exhaustively rigorous collection of material.

(1) **In antiquo carmine cum pater filio de agricultura praeciperet: hiberno pulvere verno luto grandia farra, camille, metes** (Paul. exc. Fest. p. 82.18-22 Lindsay; cf. Macr. 5.20.17f., Serv. Dan. *ad* Verg. *G.* 1.101). 'My boy, you will reap abundance of spelt in the dust of winter, in the mud of spring'.

(2) **Novum vetus vinum bibo, novo veteri morbo medeor** (Varro *Ling. Lat.* 6.21; cf. Paul. exc. Fest. p. 110.23 Lindsay). 'I drink the wine both young and old; by both young and old I am cured of sickness'.

(3) *Pueri lusu cantare solent* ['children are used to sing at play']: *rex erit qui recte faciet, qui non faciet, non erit* (Porphyrio *ad* Hor. *Epist.* 1.1.59). 'who does good will be king, who does not, will not be'. Cf. Courtney, 483f. (parody), Wille, 149, Fraenkel (ch. 5, n. 10), 365 = 18.

(4) **Ibi pastores ludos faciunt coriis Consualia** (Varro *de vita populi Romani* 1, frag. 23 Riposati). 'There the shepherds play the game <at> the Consualia <on/with> hides'. See Marquardt-Mau (n. 12), 837 n. 2 for the use of oiled bladders.

(5) *Retiario pugnanti adversus murmillonem cantatur:* **non te peto, piscem peto. quid me fugis, Galle?** (Paul. exc. Fest. p. 359.1-4). 'I'm not after you, I'm after the fish [on the *murmillo*'s helmet]; why are you running from me, Gaul [*murmillones* were originally called *Galli*]?'

(6) *Qui* [*sc. pueri*] *ludentes solent dicere* [boys at play are accustomed to say]: **quisquis ad me novissime venerit habeat scabiem.** 'Who gets to me last gets the itch', Porphyrio *ad* Hor. *Ars P.* 417. See Brink's note on this passage; Porphyrio's information derives from Suetonius' lost treatise on children's games.

(7) Children composed *ballistia* [songs to go with dances] and *cantiunculas*, 'ditties' on the warlike achievements of the emperor Aurelian. The dances were then carried out *militariter*, after the manner of soldiers. So *SHA Aurelian* 6.4: funny, clever stuff follows, perhaps too much so ever to have belonged to a real playground. No surprise for the *SHA*.

(8) Cf. above p. 37 with n. 34 for Aulus Gellius 4.5.5 *scite factus cantatusque a pueris.*

(9) Cf. above p. 38 with n. 40 for Suetonius, *Caligula* 6.1 *salva Roma, salva patria, salvus est Germanicus.*

3. Music returns to Rome

(10) Petronius 58.8 *qui de nobis longe venio, large venio? solve me.* 'I'm the one of us who comes out long, and I come out wide. Solve me.' Cf. p. 81 for riddles and p. 38 for the metre, predictably a trochaic tetrameter.

4
Culture without education; education without school

Popular culture at Rome is best understood in the context of the various ways by which it is acquired; 'education' is clearly not the right word and 'acculturation' is a specialist term with a different meaning. Most of the next three chapters will, though, be taken up by the various activities, music aside, which interacted to inform and indeed to constitute popular culture. A little recognisable education and a fair bit of fun, but surprisingly little inert, passive reception (in a modern, couch potato sense) of ready-provided mass entertainment: even the arena, after all, entailed social contact, political demonstration, betting and the strong, public, mass play of the emotions.

Take, then, military service, in times of war and peace alike: for example, Polybius refers specifically to 8,800 Roman soldiers (including 400 cavalry) stationed at Tarentum and in Sicily, at the same time, in 225 BC.[1] How much Greek did they have to learn? How much could they have learned? Clearly, enough to keep bed and cup filled, means permitting.[2] Or was there at least in some cases a more ample, inevitable acculturation? Modern analogies and ancient linguistic evidence rather suggest that this possibility was not mere sentimental opti-

4. Culture without education; education without school

mism. Seventy years ago Tenney Frank compared the republican legionary's Greek with the French that a Doughboy brought back from a necessarily shorter (1917-18) stay in Europe,[3] and the interested reader will be eager to cite full, rich confirmation from Kipling's stories and, even more, from Frank Richards' extraordinary memoir of his time as a private soldier in India.[4] Plautus' audience contains numerous veterans[5] and he uses both a number of terms from technical military language[6] and some distinctive words from the Greek of South Italy and Sicily;[7] that creates the context in which his many allusions to Greek *mores* and usage will have been understood.[8] References to Greek diet, clothes, life-style, cities and city life, geography, literature and history require a public at least partly familiar with them; such familiarity has long been thought[9] to derive chiefly from contacts between Roman army and Greek world, from a kitbag of miscellaneous notions about the Greek world brought home along with more solid booty. At the same time, we must acknowledge that there is very little Greek in the *sermo castrensis*, army Latin, at least under the empire. That may reflect the cultural geography of recruitment areas, service in areas where little Greek was spoken, and a stance of robust preference (if not a matter of actual policy) for Latin over all other languages in military speech.[10]

Emigration, immigration[11] and the continuous movement of *negotiatores*, businessmen,[12] all tended towards ample practical Hellenisation at a modest social level. We might note, among Romans in the East, one enrolled in the Athenian *ephebeia*, another runner-up in the prize for tragedy at Tanagra in 85 BC, another member of a jury at Cyrene,[13] but what is important to our enquiry is not so much active Roman participation in the cultural life of the late Hellenistic world as the slow cumulative effect of prolonged business contacts between Greeks and Romans, both in Greece and in Italy, in the context of business language[14] and the terminology of wares sold.[15] Our studies of Hellenisation at Rome have in general concentrated far too much on the aristocracy, on philosophy, on literature. In a helpfully provocative moment, however, the late Harry Jocelyn remarked that as instrument of Hellenisation a pastrycook was no less important than a philosopher.[16]

The endless discussions of the size of Rome's population are not essential to this argument;[17] the figure of 150,000 prisoners taken by Aemilius Paullus in his defeat of Macedonia (168 BC) is recorded,[18] and is likely to conceal a fairly substantial number of Macedonians actually shipped to Rome and Italy, an influx meaningless as a statistic but significant as a symbol of a continuous flow of Greek-speaking manpower into Italy. The tendency of immigrants to cluster by place of origin is familiar from our modern evidence (New York, Rome, London ...) but for ancient Rome the evidence is less clear.[19] Was an ancient *insula* (block of flats) a complete racial mix, or not? In modern Rome,[20] for what the analogy is worth, you still quite often get a dominant group in a given *palazzo* (block), from (for example) Sardinia, still deriving from the great wave of post-war immigration and a vision of (ancient) Roman landings and courtyards as the cradles of linguistic and cultural integration is not to be dismissed as fanciful. Similar acculturation may also have occurred inside a slave *familia*,[21] but since Greek was in fact the dominant language for many of the

4. Culture without education; education without school

forms of work in which Greeks, slave, freed, and free, engaged, it is eminently possible that *they* rather Hellenised their Italian (or African, Gallic, Spanish ...) neighbours.

Our very copious literary and epigraphic evidence may tend to lead us to an excessively limited definition of the Greeks' role as *vitiorum ministeria*, the work-force of the vices;[22] recent studies[23] have indeed given specificity and substance to those specialised trades in which Greeks, or at least Greeks with a natural aptitude in those directions, tended to concentrate[24] – vintners, musicians, jewellers, cooks, architects, actors, prostitutes (of whatever gender). That led naturally to a strong Greek element in the Latin terminology and to a marked element of xenophobia in the Moral Reaction.[25] To talk of luxury, or of sex, at Rome led you naturally to the use of Greek.[26] But apart from titbits and endearments, Greek had a profound impact on the language of medicine,[27] of building, and indeed of farming.[28] We should not forget those hundreds of thousands of Greek slaves who had toiled on the land – and now continued to do so in the appalling conditions of a rural *ergastulum*, or estate worked by chain-gang (itself from the Greek, *ergazein*, to toil).

The presence of Greek elements in vulgar Latin[29] entails various complications that rule out swift and simple generalisations. In documents that derive from military contexts – the two principal collections are those from Bu Njem and Vindolanda[30] – there is very little Greek influence, for reasons already discussed (see n. 10) and this same state of affairs also obtains in purely commercial contexts – like the pottery works of La Graufesenque in the Tarn valley and the wholesale trading settlement of Magdalensberg[31] in Carinthia, apart from the Greek names in current use for certain objects. Much more surprising is how little Greek influence there is in the vocabulary of the graffiti of Pompeii,[32] in sharp contrast with the world of Petronius' *Cena Trimalchionis*, a remarkably realistic portrait, so far as we can tell, of nearby Puteoli written some fifteen years before the eruption of AD 79,[33] in which the literary representation of the language used by the freedmen over dinner is often a sort of half-Greek patois.[34] Naples, on the road from Puteoli to Pompeii, was a *Graeca urbs*,[35] a real urban centre of Greek culture, where the whole way of life (*diagoge*) was still strongly Greek according to Strabo, writing under Augustus;[36] from Naples, a marked Greek influence spread widely through the Osco-Latin peoples of the hinterland. Juvenal notoriously declared to his fellow-citizens (3.60f.) that he was sick of a Greek Rome (*non possum ferre, Quirites,/ Graecam urbem*). If we were to conclude that at least in some of the cities or towns of central Italy under the early empire the dominant culture was to some extent bilingual,[37] we would not be far wrong, even though we cannot establish any sort of solid chronological structure for the growth and decline of the phenomenon.

Above all, the examples cited of significant borrowing of words are not case-studies for refined philological analysis but rather linguistic phenomena which have to be explained by some form of solid, prolonged social contact,[38] some context in which humble Romans, of whatever origin, naturally absorb Greek words. Lists of linguistic borrowings (be they unguents, undies, exotic foods or precious stones!) are profoundly exciting, for each presupposes a historical context of acculturation, a social reality towards which we are reaching.

4. Culture without education; education without school

In the Roman melting-pot, anyone could go to see Greek athletics,[39] Greek theatre, and (slightly mysterious) Greek *ludi*, possibly neither theatre nor athletics, but dance or music.[40] The theatre was indeed remarkable: twice[41] Suetonius refers to 'actors of all languages'; you don't say 'all' if you only mean 'two' and thus, apart from Latin, we have to take into account[42] stage-plays in (1) Etruscan, (2) Greek and (3) Oscan! The first is a scrap of information sent to perplex us, for Volnius 'wrote Etruscan tragedies', *tragoedias Tuscas scripsit* (Varro *Ling. Lat.* 5.55). 'In Etruscan'? 'On Etruscan topics'? When? For whom? We have really no idea. In the late first century BC, the teenage actress Eucharis Licinia had appeared on the Greek stage, *scaena Graeca*,[43] and Cicero casts doubt on the popularity of Greek actors (n. 40), yet it looks likely that such performances, known in Marius' time, went on until the Augustan period. Writing under Augustus, Strabo tells us (5.3.6) that at certain festivals poems in Oscan were still acted on stage and performed like mimes. Cicero confirms the existence of performances in Oscan,[44] presumably something much like the Atellan farce (itself a kind of *commedia dell' arte*). Were Greek plays put on for the cultivated élite and the immigrants? Was there not much text in the Oscan (?)farces, or were the theatres loyally packed with residents of Oscan origin? One can well understand farce performed in individual neighbourhoods, but less easily plays 'in Greek', if that is, literally, what Suetonius implies. Out of this morass of problems, it emerges only that some sort of popular stage performances in languages other than Latin were available in Rome in the late republic, for those who wanted – or were just curious.

The Culture of the Roman Plebs

Oscan farces may have seemed rather impenetrable to Syrian immigrants, but we are beginning to learn something of the great range of entertainments on offer, some of a surprisingly high cultural level: it will not have been easy for the man in the Roman street to avoid contact with all and every one, at least between, roughly, AD 50 and 100. These are the years for which we have most evidence for the diversity of popular entertainments available, a density of textual material (Seneca, Juvenal, Martial, Pliny, Petronius, Plutarch, Dio Chrysostom) which might lead us correctly (or wrongly; we just don't quite know) to the impression of some sort of boom in popular culture in those years.

The theatre is perhaps our focal point for considering the 'cultural education' of the *plebs*, but too much theatre could lead to quite the wrong sort of image of the whole process and for that reason we begin with some rather less obvious channels of the transmission of words, ideas, images, and stories. To begin, then, with the wandering philosopher, first attested, through a fog of obscure polemic, in Cicero's time: he writes of Epicurean followers of one Amafinius, who have 'occupied all Italy',[45] while Cassius reproaches him with 'so many country Stoics', *rusticos Stoicos*.[46] These men were the earliest forerunners of that great crowd of popular preachers of Cynicism (in particular) and Stoicism which seems to have filled Italy under the early empire.[47] Cassius' complaint defies precise definition; the phrasing may point to the countryside, literally, or to some uncouthness of style and thought. But these first hedgerow sages seem actually to have been less rare on the ground than Cicero's two references suggest, for the mime, a fundamentally popular type of theatre, at a modest

4. Culture without education; education without school

intellectual level (p. 60) seems to have been full of allusions to philosophical ideas, at least in simple formulations, with a definite vein of curiosity about Pythagoreanism.[48] And not the mime alone, for there is a good deal of philosophy, simplified but recognisable, in the graffiti of Pompeii, on metrical epitaphs, in the inscriptions of boards for *xii scripta* (p. 76f.), in proverbs, on the inscription of a Boscoreale cup and in the tipsy meditations of Trimalchio's guests.[49]

Philosophers, and poets. The poets are no less problematic, for what we know of them depends largely upon evidence from the satirists who will not tell us what percentage of the *plebs* could hear them,[50] though I have wondered whether they did not also recite better poets' pieces when they ran out of their own and whether their labours might help to explain in part the diffusion of metrical graffiti and inscriptions (cf. p. 64).[51] It suits the satirists to suggest that such poets were pretty much omnipresent, in the markets, in the baths, in the Circus Maximus and even, according to Martial, in pursuit of a more captive audience in the multi-seater latrines.[52] Elsewhere, of course, you were freer to escape the wandering versifier, but their very existence confirms a basic and neglected distinction between contact with literature, generously defined, and direct contact with written texts (of some sort). Indeed scholars have tended to underestimate the contexts in which a plebeian might encounter (willy-nilly, even) literature as performance.[53] During the *cena Trimalchionis*, wandering *Homeristae* performed travesties of the epics, such as survive on papyrus scraps;[54] the master of the house himself, in some way aware of a fashion becoming daily more fashionable for improvised poetic composition,[55] has a go at emulating, in his own way, such masters of the art as that Archias whom Cicero defended and the poet Statius[56] and that a rich freedman might do so does not seem absurd to Petronius. If even Trimalchio might be represented thus, we could begin to wonder[57] what might, realistically, have happened at a social reunion of the senior clerks of some imperial secretariat.

If we mount to slightly more 'respectable' levels of performance, we are beset by an abundance of evidence: thus, dramatic performances of Virgil's *Bucolics* began even during the poet's lifetime[58] and continued down to the time of St Augustine,[59] not to mention pantomimes (see below, p. 15) on Virgilian themes.[60] Public readings from the *Aeneid* went on in Rome until the seventh century AD. But almost more surprising is the detail preserved for us by Aulus Gellius, that there was a reading of the *Annals* of Ennius in the theatre of Puteoli, a busy port and commercial centre, but set on a coastline sought-after for fashionable holidays and graced by the presence of occasional distinguished philosophers.[61] The choice of Ennius, rather than Virgil, makes a point, clearly, at the height of the Romans' passion for their archaic literary past, but it is the choice of a theatre[62] rather than the much smaller *odeion* that strikes the reader: this was perforce a performance that expected the sort of numbers that might ordinarily come to a pantomime. We can easily imagine Ovid's *Heroides* on the stage, either as some form of dramatic reading of the actual text or as the basis for a pantomime.[63] It is easy enough to imagine the popular appeal that Virgil, even Ovid might have continued to exercise (cf. Shakespeare, or Verdi in Italy). Readings of Statius' *Thebaid* and *Achilleid*[64] had, I suspect, much more of an élite appeal, but the fact remains that such

4. Culture without education; education without school

public readings did exist and the text of Statius was offered for the enjoyment of anyone willing to enter the auditorium (or to peer round the doors), illiterates not excluded. That goes for any reading of any author, of course.[65]

A remark made by Apuleius has not received due attention: if you go to the *odeion* (?),[66] you will see a mime, a ropewalker, a juggler, a comedy, a tragedy, or a philosophical discourse. Was the whole programme known in its entirety to the whole audience before the show began? It is odd that we have lots of gladiatorial programmes,[67] and even some lists of market-days in the towns of a given area,[68] but no hint – unless I have been looking in the wrong places for ten years – at the form or content of the programme for a theatre or *odeion*.[69] Recent discussions of what was offered in the theatres of Pompeii and Ostia take refuge in general statements;[70] Dio Cassius tells us that under Commodus a prostitute dressed as a leopard was on show in the Ostia theatre.[71] And that is all.

Recently, the *circulator* has been tried out as a magic key to unlock several mysteries of Roman literary history (cf. p. 98f.);[72] the bare facts, though, are interesting enough: the *circulator* is a street entertainer or busker who draws about him a *circulus*, even in the Forum;[73] the *circulus* is, literally, the little circle of hearers and they are held by a wide variety of turns;[74] such *circulatores* would seem, naturally, a key element in any definition of the 'culture of the common people', but when a *circulator* reads a text, prose or poetry, sings, or recounts a myth,[75] he acts as a link between his hearers and the world of theatre and books, after the manner of the actor, or the professional *lector* (reader), or the *aretalogus* (storyteller; literally, 'teller of marvels').[76]

The Culture of the Roman Plebs

By this point, we may be a little less disconcerted by the idea that the Roman theatre might have had (not deliberately, of course!) some kind of actual pedagogic function. Thus we return to the public of Plautus and Terence in the playwrights' lifetime and to the revival of second-century drama of which Cicero tells us so much; for the period 210-160 BC, we have the texts of the plays and virtually nothing else;[77] for the revivals, anything but the texts; as a result, the social history of the Roman theatre is not easily written.[78] The plebeian who really wanted to see *Miles Gloriosus* or *Eunuchus* was able to do so, though perhaps not always at the first performance (p. 13). The public was rich and varied, including (ex-)soldiers, women, children, nurses, tarts, slaves, magistrates' escorts.[79] However, that at least a good part of the audience understood a fair bit of Greek mythology is a necessary inference from the allusions in the texts and from the extravagant variations upon more orthodox versions of familiar myths.[80] Without widespread understanding of the originals, far too large a part of the mythological references would have been little more than a tedious show of useless erudition, and such understanding is easily explained if the public of comedy also regularly frequented the tragic theatre.[81] Plautus *Bacchides* 925ff. presupposes Ennius' *Andromache*, and indeed verse 933 actually cites the earlier play. Nor should we forget either mythological art (p. 90) or epic poetry,[82] publicised by *circulatores* or public readings, though neither seems remotely as credible a means of painless mass coaching in Greek myth as a programme of regular visits to the theatre.

This is not to suggest that the mass public went to the theatre so as to learn Greek myth. There were indeed attrac-

4. Culture without education; education without school

tions of a very different order, but there is no profound incompatibility between unblushing delight taken in the most lurid special effects, flames, storms, battles, droves of animals, ghosts[83] and a genuine love for the old tragedies. Had Aristotle lived to see Ennius performed at Rome, he might not have written of the collective purging of the spectators' emotions,[84] but the cool observer could hardly have failed to miss a deep and genuine enthusiasm, perhaps seen most clearly in the revivals of the Ciceronian age: when Pompey's theatre was opened in 55 BC, Accius' *Clytemnestra* and (?)Naevius' *Equus Troianus* were performed, with, predictably, lavish special effects,[85] spectacular proof of a deep-rooted cultural conservatism.

It should not be thought that aristocratic magistrates were stuffing unwelcome old plays into the maws of a reluctant public; such plays can hardly have been chosen at random, or to bore the audience, and some degree of active concern to meet popular taste is overwhelmingly likely, even though the conventional view of the outlay entailed as being an investment towards re-election is now vigorously challenged.[86] The ample scale of the late-republican revivals of comedy and tragedy meant, naturally, that just as 150 years before, tragedy taught the public the mythology that comedy presupposed; that public was moreover ever more familiar with the Greek world of the comedies thanks of course to immigration, to military service, and to commerce. But it is generally agreed that this revived enthusiasm for the old plays began to decline very noticeably in the first years of the empire[87] and this decline went hand in hand with an altogether new popular enthusiasm for the pantomime, a ballet for soloists, with a strong mimic element, accompanied by a text performed by the chorus.[88] It is very likely that the new form – new, that is, at Rome[89] – simply pushed out the old. Pantomime clearly contained far less text than traditional tragedy and comedy and made less strictly intellectual demands upon its public, but that reduction entailed no corresponding loss of the ability to arouse (and to satisfy) strong collective emotional reactions or to take root as strongly as the old plays had done in the social memory. The titles of very numerous pantomimes on mythological themes are preserved.[90] The popularity of the genre lasted half a millennium,[91] roughly, on a prodigious scale:[92] its spread was unlimited and effectively unchallenged (Caesarius after all kept trying, to little effect, p. 16f.); that entailed the mass diffusion of the mythological stories retold and the general memorisation, under ideal circumstances, of the songs (p. 15).

But if we return to the late republic and early empire, it would be quite wrong to imagine that a popular audience reacted only when faced with lurid effects and extravagant emotionality. We have seen that there was a philosophical vein even on gaming-boards and in the mime (p. 55); a certain ethical severity on the comic and tragic stage was also appreciated[93] (even if not always followed at home); a good *sententia*, the pithy formulation of a moral truth, aroused applause;[94] grief could spread throughout the auditorium;[95] the magnanimity of Orestes and Pylades in Pacuvius' *Chryse* aroused 'the greatest expressions of admiration', *admirationes maximas*, and the audience stood to applaud.[96] This is not the moment to attribute to the Roman *plebs* widespread and profound moral seriousness, or a universal interest in abstract

4. Culture without education; education without school

thought,[97] but there does really seem to be evidence to confirm a certain general interest in moral or ethical issues, so long as they were pithily expressed and not too shocking. The mime also offered its audience sex in abundance (p. 80); a single, Roman, public relished both the elevated and the horizontal.

That vast public in the Roman world unable, for whatever reason, or (though formally literate) unwilling to read those prose and verse texts which have survived down to modern times (which are largely of high literature and of fine quality) nevertheless brought home a wide and varied amalgam of words and notions heard in the street (p. 98), in the inn (p. 15), in the theatre (*ib*.), at a banquet of his *collegium* (p. 33): None of this of course was perforce solidly memorised or deeply absorbed, but what stuck was the result of mass culture, of a kind, was a real Roman social memory, however barren, slender, pre-modern. There emerge both some rather surprising links (cf. further ch. 5) with the cultural world of the élite and some perhaps less expected distancing (in a superior direction!) from the glorious portrait, parody, travesty of nouveau riche *mores* that we get in Petronius' *Cena Trimalchionis*.

But I have no desire to offer an impression of the Roman *plebs* as prim and virtuous in their theatregoing;[98] at most, I offer some evidence to be borne in mind which should suggest a certain open-mindedness on popular tastes, and not always towards the low and lewd. To conclude this chapter, though, we must look at the classic anecdotes, however tricky to interpret,[99] which have hitherto served to block attempts to upgrade our views of popular preferences in Rome's theatres.

The theatre public's show-stopping cries of 'Bears, bears,

now' or 'Stop; bring on the boxers', or 'Gladiators!!!' or even 'We want tightrope-walkers' still ring in our ears;[100] we do not know if the scenes were unusual, or typical, organised or spontaneous, of political origin (to embarrass the magistrate responsible for the show), or cultural (a straight protest against tedium, a call for simple fun). But it is worth looking briefly at the alternatives requested to see what elucidation of the scenes they offer. Bears[101] and tightrope-walkers do not conventionally belong to the theatre at all; their affinity is rather with the world of *circulatores*, buskers or travelling entertainers (p. 98). There are tightrope-walkers in Horace, but he does not locate them; indeed they are first solidly attested in a theatre at the time of St Augustine.[102] And that cry for bears is not attested quite as solidly as we might wish, for behind Horace's *aut ursum aut pugiles*, there lurk the eagerly-awaited boxers of Terence *Hecyra* 33, onto whom Horace, who knew and loved his Terence, has stitched bruin,[103] by way of a modest variation or 'improvement'. Boxers likewise stagger a little when examined: apparently coming from Etruria, they had long been known at Rome, and belong solidly to the world of *ludi publici* or to the semi-organised brawling of the back streets.[104] Gladiators, in turn, expected by the *Hecyra*'s public (or so the rumour went) on the second performance (38ff.), belong originally to improvised enclosures in the Forum and then to amphitheatres, not theatres.[105] Terence seems (as does Horace, if his evidence is to be treated as independent) to be lamenting behaviour by a crowd determined upon entertainment which they could never hope to get, however long they sat and booed, in their theatre. A preference for bears over the *Hecyra* might even count as fair criticism, were the two

4. Culture without education; education without school

entertainments comparable; as it is, try to imagine the expression of a preference for baseball over Bach in the auditorium of your choice. The crowd bawls very deliberately for the impossible, to create chaos and to prevent the performance; Terence *was* appreciated in his age, and *Hecyra* is not so profoundly inferior to *Andria* and *Eunuchus* (the favourites).[106] There is something else going on that we have lost: word has gone out to block the performance and to make it look good. Why, we do not know; the key to the episode, whether political, social, financial or literary, is lost.

5

Fun for all

If you follow Latin literature (as conventionally understood) on its (arguably downhill) path towards popular culture, you are struck, amid much else, by a marked and initially disconcerting increase of anonymity. Many names of actors and pantomimes are known,[1] whereas if you ask who wrote the songs sung in the sausage-shops of Bordeaux (p. 137, n. 4), or indeed of Rome, not to mention theatre-songs, triumph-chants, salacious epigrams on the vices of consuls and emperors, and unsigned metrical epitaphs, along with those hypothetical but seductive pattern-books[2] of epitaphs which probably hung from nails in the corners of many stonecutters' workshops across the empire and, lastly, those thousands of graffiti, many in verse and quite a few genuinely witty, recovered from the walls of Pompeii[3] and elsewhere, ephemera fossilised in the hands of epigraphists, there are no named authors, but at last a few fairly persuasive hypotheses. I had thought not so much of signed epitaphs[4] (for such authors are not necessarily authors by trade) as of the not very many epitaphs we have of 'So-and-so, poet',[5] that is to say one who exercised the business of being a local poet (and perhaps never wrote that vast epic upon the defeat of Boadicea). 'Poet' that is, as a recognisable label under which to pass a life; perhaps

5. Fun for all

too a part-time label, as the analogy of *Inscr. Lat. Sel.* 7763 might suggest: a schoolteacher who drew up wills after work.[6] That does not really bring us any closer to understanding just *who* really prepared for mass use the wonderful range of chants, insults, acclamations and 'songs', whose potential for being organised and launched we have already discussed (p. 38f.). Certainly under the empire, our really quite substantial surviving remains of – let us call it, the ephemeral poetry of protest, show definite, visible traces of linguistic and metrical skill,[7] which do suggest the activity of one or more expert hands in preparation before they were put into circulation. Another line of approach, potentially most rewarding, lies in the metrical unity (p. 38) of *carmina triumphalia*, riddles,[8] children's songs (p. 46) and numerous proverbs,[9] enriched by alliteration, rhyme, wordplay and the like: lines wonderfully well-suited to memorisation and performance, as we have seen reason to suspect.[10] It may seem paradoxical, but while we have a fair idea of what there was in the 'social memory'[11] of the Roman *plebs*, we are only now trying to work out how that memory was awakened and fed; 'alternatives to literacy' (p. 48ff.) are not easy to track down for a society we have now to try to understand chiefly on the basis on written materials.

We were raised on 'the cultural horizons of the aristocracy',[12] and it comes naturally still to Roman historians to write (I select, strenuously) 'there was no such thing as "popular literature" in the Roman empire'[13] or 'how far down the ladder one has to go before reaching those to whom books were wholly inaccessible it is hard to say';[14] in such a context, it would seem natural to study only (for example) the Hellenisation of the super-literate.[15] But there have now been a few

The Culture of the Roman Plebs

faint utterances of protest against this apparently unchallengeable chorus of received wisdom,[16] and it might at last be time to offer a first tentative sketch to define the Romans' 'culture of the underprivileged'.[17]

There is, behind the quotations just offered, a widely-credited model of Roman cultural life which still haunts our studies: of an unquestionable and irreversible hierarchy, with, in the remote distance at the top end, an aristocratic minority which exercises complete control, politically, economically, and therefore culturally. This minority enjoys full and instant access to all literary forms and indeed controls most aspects of literary production, while the vast majority is bullied, exploited, poor and therefore naturally condemned by economic circumstances, aristocratic bullying and political manipulation to – if not illiteracy proper,[18] then at least to a profound degree of intellectual impoverishment inevitably imposed by the accumulation of political and financial handicaps, with, as an inescapable result, ignorance of political life and further electoral manipulation. We might be allowed to except a handful of the 'poor but able' – grammarians, vets, accountants and surveyors[19] – but they are not thought seriously to affect the vast Us/Them divide. Those who have read this far will realise that that such a model is losing its capacity to convince – and not me alone (cf. n. 16). The *plebs* are re-acquiring a powerful role in late republican politics (p. 20ff.), and not without difficulty there begin to emerge the outlines of a 'parallel' culture, in its own way rich, varied and robustly vigorous: it has little enough to do with those literary texts which have bequeathed to us such a magnificent set of cultural and social blinkers (p. 28ff.), but rests rather on theatre, games in various

5. Fun for all

senses, music, songs, dance, memory and has amply demonstrated its ability to survive almost unaltered at least into late antiquity (p. 23f.). Horace's inifinitely memorable Volteius Mena (p. 28) was not, I suspect, fascinated by the subtleties of elegiac diction, nor by the Greek erudition hidden in the texts of Livius Andronicus and Naevius,[20] but that did not condemn him to a bottomless pit of boundless cultural inferiority. Horace tells us (*Epist.* 1.7.59) that Volteius enjoyed the *ludi*; I could believe that such a man might have visited the theatre, have enjoyed the mime, have sung songs as he cleaned his fingernails, even have visited a dramatic performance of that recent hit, Virgil's *Bucolics*. At dinner with Marcius Philippus, why should he not have quoted some *carmina triumphalia*, some irreverent political epigrams, even a handful of cherished couplets of Catullus?[21] Cicero's speeches to a popular audience reveal after all, flatteries apart, a thoughtful and considered sense of their actual intelligence and knowledge (p. 85f.).

Hitherto, we have not considered the Romans' ample and varied 'common fund' or 'middle ground'[22] not only of entertainments both public and private but of activities not unreasonably to be described as 'cultural' and enjoyed at all levels of society. No optimistic, democratic hypothesis, this: at the theatre (amphitheatre, circus) there was division of the seating by status, grimly considered, then reconsidered, and meticulously prescribed,[23] a visible discrimination rendered yet more important by the extraordinary popularity and huge crowds these occasions could attract, but all were united by venue and by the spectacle, whether race, fight or play: tarts and empresses could share, and were seen to share emotions, in public, even though huge variations in upbringing and education will have led to some variations even in reaction to the unifying spectacle. Augustus was careful not to repeat Caesar's mistake of taking official business to the various entertainments;[24] he went to be seen, and apparently to relish too. Equality before the spectacle might seem less dramatic, though, than equality in the water: an extreme sign of imperial *comitas*, graciousness, was to visit the public baths;[25] no doubt status could even there be expressed by towels, nails, haircut, grooming, number of attendants, comportment, to be weighed up against the simple facts of shared nudity and shared water.

Of course similarly nuanced and stratified reaction will emerge, at whatever entertainment, game or cultural experience we choose to look. For though the soldier after his couple of years in garrison at Tarentum (p. 48) is likely to be a bilingual, in some sense, he is not to be compared to Publius Licinius Crassus Mucianus, consul 131 BC, who is said to have had perfect command of five versions (*genera*) of Greek: classical, *koine* (standard post-Classical usage), and three dialects, I imagine.[26] The amount of Greek (words, things, ideas) in Plautus' plays shows that he did not reckon the soldier a spectator at home solely and exclusively in the Roman world (p. 49). Stratification emerges very clearly in the unlikely terrain of works on farming: Virgil's *Georgics* are not about farming at all, in a didactic sense, as an infinitely refined and difficult poem about the country and about ethical values.[27] They contain a little good counsel for the farmer, unhelpfully arranged. Varro's *Res Rusticae* were written, I suspect, for a class of new proprietors, men who had emerged on top after the civil wars and proscriptions and wanted to make the most

5. Fun for all

of their new holdings, though ignorant of the countryside, of the technical jargon, of the right way to go about doing things, and perhaps above all of the gentle art of not leaving everything in the bailiff's hands.[28] Moving down, we come to the head-goatherds (*magistri pecoris*) to whom Varro refers (*Res rust.* 2.3.8), who are to carry written instructions (*quaedam scripta*) to consult in case of wounds or sickness among their beasts. As a result, a wide range of manuals (on farming, accountancy, veterinary medicine, and so on) at all cultural and economic levels were available.[29]

The wide range of Latin proverbs presupposes, as has been clear for a while, an analogous range in the level of their users;[30] expressions like 'mules in the ditch' or 'playing *morra*[31] in the dark' do clearly imply a cultural background markedly different from 'harder than adamant' or 'Hyblaean bees'. But we need to look at such hierarchies with some degree of scepticism and humanity, to take account of the landowner who enjoyed his farm bailiff's colourful speech,[32] or the dealer in used clothes (it is hard to forget Volteius Mena) who happened to be in the theatre when Ovid's *Heroides* were performed (p. 56) and remained struck by the comparison (2.137) with the hardness of adamant. We are not, therefore, going to be able to shuffle and sort all our proverbs by income brackets.

Cicero lavished heavy mockery upon a kind of dramatic banquet in which Euripides, Menander, Socrates and Epicurus took part, though not, apparently, all at once:[33] 'figures separated not by years but by centuries' he grumbled, 'an author no less ignorant than his public'. And so on. But if the anachronism had actually been the key to the whole comical, and promising, encounter? The occasionally humourless statesman may simply have preferred to miss the point. Under Tiberius, one Asellius Sabinus was richly rewarded by a delighted emperor for his humorous dialogue between a mushroom, a figpicker, an oyster and a thrush;[34] if you want to argue from, or for, cultural hierarchies, there are problems when the emperor himself is a man of limited, even of coarse tastes.[35]

Even without so much as sketching a social stratification of Roman humour, it will soon become clear enough that several 'popular' forms of humour enjoyed surprising upward mobility. The *parasitus*, or professional scrounger, in Plautus' *Persa* claims to have a hamper full of books of jokes;[36] just possibly such books reflect actual Roman usage (and in that case they will hardly have been for general circulation), but more probably they reflect upon the *parasitus*' lack of mother wit.[37] More promisingly, the coarse humour of the *scurra*, or buffoon[38] seems to have been adopted (at least that is what our possibly biased sources claim) by a number of minor figures in the political life of the late republic,[39] such as Sextus Naevius, *scurra* and auctioneer, adversary of the Quinctius whom Cicero defended in his first surviving speech,[40] or Granius, both auctioneer and *familiaris*, companion of Crassus the orator (father of the triumvir): Granius' wit Cicero analyses favourably in the *De oratore*.[41] Let us not forget that the *scurra* Sarmentus is part of Maecenas' suite, along with Horace, Virgil, Plotius and Varius, on their famous journey to Brundisium. Horace offers us a literary reworking of his clash with the Oscan, let us call him, stand-up comic Messius Cicirrus.[42] Clearly, the context is significant: Horace presents Sarmentus as a sort of (perfectly acceptable) 'court buffoon' in a text

5. Fun for all

which clearly enough tries to idealise the life-style of Maecenas and his companions.[43] Statesmen are to be seen to enjoy the company of leading poets, and likewise of stand-up comics.

A century passes, and we reach Petronius: my attempt to explain that the humour of the freedmen in the *Cena* is portrayed as *not* altogether deserving of the élite reader's lofty contempt has been received quite generously:[44] Petronius has indeed a certain – slightly appalled, perhaps – sympathy with the freedmen and if we leap to the usual conclusion that the 'educated reader' (even worse, the reader at court) will, naturally, of course, have found the entire episode grotesque and boorish in tone, then we risk debasing and trivialising the entire episode. The play of sympathies and satire is intricate and merits reading as such. There is no doubting that the freedmen are represented as truly loving their language and way of speaking; their relish for life and for words far outstrips their grammar.[45] They are not represented as linguistically handicapped or economically disadvantaged by their cultural backwardness and the entertainments offered at dinner make us suspect that Trimalchio has heard how things are done in the real, cultivated world and seeks if not to imitate that world, then to show that he is well able to provide the same sort of thing. Thus he knows – not clearly or correctly, but he knows – that during and after dinner all his guests shall enjoy an entertainment, *acroama*, or indeed several, and that in this context, actors are much appreciated.[46] Trimalchio's *acroamata* constitute a sort of heroic approximation to polite usage; 'imitation' might suggest a certain seriousness of intent which I am not sure he is to be allowed. Because of the odd, confused way in which our sources are transmitted, we find that chance has focused our attention on two opposed cultural extremes, the world of Trimalchio and, in contrast, that monument to commitment, seriousness and correct good taste which we find in Pliny's *Letters* or Plutarch's *Quaestiones conviviales*.[47] Thus, on account of the hand of chance in transmitting our evidence, we tend to forget that between the extremes there once ran a long sequence of gently declining (or ascending) cultural correctness, represented by (for example) the banquets of the *collegia* (p. 33), or the centurions' mess in a legionary camp (p. 110). Quite serious, culturally, quite ambitious – or not; there are too many uncertainties that make it impossible for us to guess or to generalise. But the existence of many kinds of troupe of travelling actors in the Hellenistic and Roman worlds[48] makes it possible for us to view in slightly more concrete terms the existence of a long sliding scale of 'cultural values' on which a shrewd troupe of actors could judge upon the moment the precise level at which they would be performing that evening, at least if all went according to plan.

Appendix: the issue of literacy

An acute reader of Horsfall (1995) remarked to me that I had said nothing about literacy. Was the culture of the *plebs* literate or not? It was not a text-based culture, and rested upon memory rather than active literacy (whether as writer or as reader); the latter was indeed, if I am at all right, in some measure irrelevant. So, in passing, Horsfall (1998). It was a great merit of W.V. Harris' book of 1989 to open up energetic debate on the issue of literacy at Rome; Horsfall (1991) is one

5. Fun for all

of a number of responses gathered in a single volume while Thomas (1992), 158ff. presumably appeared too soon to realise how controversial the issue had become. Harris, in terms of sociology and statistics, makes a very powerful case for a strikingly low level of literacy in the period under discussion, while I suggested that such an approach inevitably skewed, and was skewed by the peculiar state of our (ample) evidence and the way it was transmitted. Now that the passion seems to have gone out of the discussion, we may even wonder whether any real progress was made, except in bringing a lot of evidence to more general notice; see e.g. J. Bodel in (ed. J.B.) *Epigraphic evidence* (London 2001), 15f. for a polite summary. More evidence has come to hand (and of course yet more will be uncovered, thanks to excavations and by sitting in libraries!): the acute reader cited above (Nicholas Purcell) drew my attention to Tac. *Ann.* 16.22, the *acta diurna* read in the provinces and in the army to find out what Thrasea Paetus did not do. So too, the recently-published *S.C. de Pisone patre* contains elaborate provisions for its publication throughout cities, provinces and legions (lines 170ff.; see e.g. H. Flower, *Class. Ant.* 17 (1998), 156f.). But any two competent players starting from precisely these positions on this particular intellectual chessboard will necessarily draw. Neither text specifies the scale of its anticipated readership (cf. Thomas (1992), 164f. for an introduction to the issue of the publication of official documents). The scale of public meetings in the Forum is not at all clear (p. 87); the scale of the anticipated readership of publicly-posted documents in the city of Rome is equally uncertain (cf. Horsfall (1991), 70). The dramatic descriptions of crowds 'reading the lists of the names of the proscribed' do not specify how large a proportion of the crowd could see the list, or could read it if they could see it (Horsfall (1991), 70, M. Corbier, in *L'Urbs* (*Coll. Ec. Fr. Rome*, Roma 1987), 43ff., Dio Cassius frag. 109.14 (Loeb ed., vol. 2, 492ff.); cf. Nepos, *Atticus* 10.4 with my note, Oxford 1989). But active participation in political life in the city requires, in practice, minimal literacy (Millar (1998), 130f., Harris (1989), 167ff., Nicolet (1976), 333ff., E.E. Best, *Historia* 23 (1974), 428ff., L.R. Taylor, *Roman voting assemblies* (Ann Arbor 1966), 34ff.), while Mouritsen (2001), 37, n. 75 forgets how very little literacy was required to vote and thus dismisses far too swiftly the 'illiterate masses of Rome', who needed only to remember a couple of letters or to stick closely to their friends. Naturally, the literate could take a more informed role, but their presence at votes and elections cannot be quantified and I have preferred not to try to introduce the factor of literacy in our study of a fundamentally oral (and even memory-based) popular culture.

6

To help pass the time

If, therefore, the humour of Trimalchio's guests is not incompatible with that of Petronius' readers, along with theatre, amphitheatre and circus, where site and show unite all those present (p. 67), it may stand as yet another element of some kind (at least in a wide sense) of 'common fund' of culture.[1] This chapter continues to seek out venues in which some Volteius Mena could (and sometimes did) have fun alongside an ex-consul. Cicero did indeed speak ill, consistently enough, of the mime,[2] but that reveals him as less tolerant and more of a snob than certain other very distinguished senators of the period.[3] He was, in short, irrelevant, out of step with a general passion. These passions, of which the 'common fund' was made up, were of fundamental importance not just as occasions to visit and view, but as topics of passionate, partisan conversation at all levels: thus when Horace makes a show of revealing to his readers the topics of his first conversations with Maecenas during their travels together, he teases us by specifying 'The Weather', 'The Time' and 'Is Gallina the Thracian a match for the Syrian?'.[4] And not only Maecenas, with Horace, but Echion the rag-dealer in Petronius, who discusses a forthcoming gladiatorial *munus* at length.[5] A risk, if you are a philosopher, and the man with whom you enter into conversation wants to talk about gladiators or horses,[6] another topic dear (though less so) to the freedmen in the *Cena Trimalchionis*.[7]

The extraordinary enthusiasm for the arena at Pompeii and among the traders at Magdalensberg (p. 51) has often been noted.[8] We have also noted the socially widespread enthusiasm for song, music and dance (p. 31ff.) and the general appeal of the *scurra*, or stand-up comic; indeed, the full catalogue of all the elements which made up the 'common fund' at Rome might be extended to imposing length, but the topic of what all (or nearly all) Romans enjoyed in their spare time, largely neglected by scholars,[9] does not naturally lend itself to exhaustive treatment and I prefer to sketch some outlines of the topic and to dwell on a few particularly interesting elements. Notoriously, Trimalchio played at ball before dinner; compare, if you will (and the list could be drawn out further) Julius Caesar, the younger Pliny, Cicero (perhaps), Augustus, the younger Cato, Sextus Titius, Vestricius Spurinna, C. Calpurnius Piso and the professional star, Urso.[10] Several types of ball-game are known,[11] but it would be tiresome to distinguish them.

More familiar are dicing (*alea*) and the whole range of table-games for which dice were used, notably *xii scripta*, an identifiable ancestor of backgammon; note that modern Greek *tavli*, not to mention Arabic *tawulah*, backgammon, derive from Latin *tabula*, board. Not all the identifications made between the games described by authors and the archaeological and epigraphic remains are entirely convincing and not all those who write on the topic are familiar with the main historical classifications of board-games.[12] It is, though, certain that the Romans played not only in taverns but in every

6. To help pass the time

corner of the city of Rome,[13] and throughout the empire (for Jerusalem, cf. p. 114). The evidence for Rome has recently been surveyed admirably by Nicholas Purcell. The literary evidence is confirmed by the number of boards found all over the city, in Italy, North Africa, and the north-west of the empire (Purcell, 18f.); I have had to manhandle one which in its prime had weighed 300 lbs (suggestive of the chessboards in European parks); others were made for travel.[14] A popular passion, clearly, and one widespread in taverns and also in the army, at the foot of the Cross and in barracks on Hadrian's Wall;[15] in the palace, likewise, for on the heels of such distinguished players as Catiline and Mark Antony, note Augustus, Caligula, Nero, and, above all, Claudius.[16]

In the first century AD, rich young aristocrats, not to mention the odd Bad Emperor, took a sort of pleasure in sharing the life of the *plebs* in the city of Rome; these drunken voyages of exploration through a new range of simpler vices[17] do not count as evidence in favour of an enlarged 'common fund', any more than does the custom of mixing guests from all social levels at dinner,[18] sometimes, but not always undertaken from a spiteful delight in provoking unease and confusion.[19] As hard evidence, the accusations often made against political foes that they frequented low taverns (p. 153, n. 17) likewise leave much to be desired.

Let us briefly imagine the scene, however, in the one tavern of some small port far down the Adriatic coast of Italy; blocked by unfavourable winds, we find thrown into each other's company for several days an importer of *garum* (fish sauce, made from rotting entrails, similar to that now imported from the Philippines), a senator, a centurion, and the poet Horace

The Culture of the Roman Plebs

(the list, clearly, is easily extended): what do they do to pass four days together? It should at least be clear by now that there is no fixed correspondence between high rank and high-mindedness; note too that there are no professional aides to culture present, no grammarians, copyists, or readers, no librarians or papyrus-repairers, men whose very existence depended on the productive perpetuation of serious literary culture.[20] We would also do well to recall the amply-attested simple tastes of certain famous public figures (p. 70): Augustus is perhaps the most interesting, and best-documented, case.[21] Some time c. 1988 I recall seeing a front-page newspaper photograph of Giulio Andreotti, then as often prime minister of Italy, returning from – might it have been Portugal, in company of the national football team. Andreotti, who has also contributed to Ciceronian studies, was playing cards with the footballers. Was this subtly calculated populism or a harmless way of passing a couple of hours, or both? Maecenas took care that it should be known that he enjoyed the company of a *scurra* (p. 70f.) when *he* travelled and likewise some mild exercise in Horace's company on the Campus Martius.[22] Augustus would have been the easiest of additions to the company, for, along with the company of Virgil and Horace, he enjoyed a tune, dice, ballgames, fishing, games with nuts, playing with small children, watching boxing, storytellers (of various kinds), and buskers.[23]

But perhaps the evidence of Pliny the Younger is more impressive, in view of his normal commitment to remorseless cultural seriousness (p. 72): in order to tell a good (and contemporary) anecdote (something he in fact did often and very well), he tells his friend Calvisius 'get your copper ready

6. To help pass the time

and you'll hear a tale of gold':[24] that has to be the cry of professional storytellers (p. 98), who busked with a joke (in this case a joke from Homer)[25] to keep their boxes filled, and it deserves to be added to our little collection of Roman street-cries (p. 43). Pliny tells the story of the boy and the dolphin[26] as one that he'd heard at dinner, while the guests on all sides recounted wonders (tall stories, we might say), *dum ... varia miracula hinc inde referuntur*. When he asks his friend Licinius Sura what he thinks of ghosts,[27] he asks as one convinced, in this case by the story of what had happened to Curtius Rufus.[28]

Naturally, our quartet stuck in the harbour bar could have gambled, or played catch. They could also have told stories, very possibly blue, as were appreciated at all levels: what changed with the environment (the Senate, or a school of declamation, say) was not so much the topics permitted (no taboos, that one can see), as the language that might be used: a number of registers of obscenity have been identified, and something can even be said about variations of lexicon by social level, by age and sex of speaker/audience, by context and by attitude.[29] When Octavian chose to say *exactly* what he thought of Mark Antony, he used language familiar from the walls of Pompeii.[30] To return to our Apulian bar, some unwritten laws on levels of plain speaking presumably applied in socially mixed conversation, without women present, in a public place, though we have no idea what the precise 'laws' in question were! Pornography written as such did exist, remote though it is from the expertly-told dirty story and little though we know of it and its readers: Tiberius was said to enjoy it, but his name attracted that sort of attribution;[31] a medical treatise proposes the therapeutic use of porn in the case of failing sexual powers,[32] and the Parthians, according to Plutarch, were shocked (or pretended to be) by the 'Milesian tales' of Aristides, found among the booty after the Romans' defeat at Carrhae in 53 BC.[33] In the mime, actresses might undress, all the way, even;[34] there might be a bed on stage, and sexual acts, not always necessarily feigned, were permitted;[35] in the language of the fragments, predictably, there were no restrictions on primary obscenity.[36] That does not prove that a senator would necessarily feel free to use the full range of primary obscenities in the company of a *garum*-seller, or vice versa.

That brings us very close to the familiar elements of wonder and the fabulous (*mirabilia, thaumata*) that we find in paradoxography (collections of surprising 'facts'), in natural history, geography and history (or at least round history's less grave and more lurid fringes, as two exceptional papers, in English, by Emilio Gabba have made clear[37]). Let us start further down the ladder: in Petronius, we find the novella of the werewolf told by Niceros and that of the witches by Trimalchio himself; the 'Milesian tale' of the ephebe of Pergamum has no context, while that of the widow of Ephesus is told during a sea-voyage and the sailors welcome it with marked enthusiasm.[38] Perhaps the most interesting instance of an inset tale in Petronius is that of the unbreakable glass, 'invented under Tiberius': this 'natural wonder', as told by Trimalchio is a travesty of a known anecdotic tradition, as we see from the 'flexible glass under Tiberius' that we find in the elder Pliny and the story in Cassius Dio of the miraculous repair of a cup of crystal, at the same period.[39] We do thus have a continuous chain of association, at least this once, between

6. To help pass the time

conventional history and the sort of anecdote that could be represented as fit for telling at a gross dinner of nouveaux riches at Puteoli.

It might be well to return for a moment to proverbs;[40] we have seen that there are numerous social levels to be distinguished within the whole patrimony of Latin proverbs, but the actual use of proverbial expressions in conversation seems to have been universal, attested as it is from Julius Caesar to Trimalchio and his friends.[41] One might begin to wonder whether some aspects of the 'common fund' actually belonged to a 'lowest common denominator' at the level of lullabies, nursery wisdom and certain types of folktale about witches and bogeymen.[42] Stories of bogeys are actually criticised by Quintilian and Tacitus and we might even suspect that the infant Tacitus had quivered with alarm in his nurse's lap on hearing of the Lamia.[43] Riddles belong at the same sort of cultural level: Plutarch says that they belong in the world of the 'coarse and unlettered' (*phortikoi kai aphilologoi*, Mor. 673A); after dinner (are we at Rome or in Greece? It is not clear,[44] so this is not necessarily a clue to the banquets of the *collegia*) they turn to riddles and, well, riddles (for a *griphos* is much like an *ainigma*!) and to correspondences between numbers and letters.[45] Riddles spread wide, in the *cena Trimalchionis*, on the walls of Pompeii, and behind a number of familiar proverbs,[46] but they also 'belong' in the world of high literature, on the lips of Virgil's shepherds and at least in the more elaborate, worked-up versions we have of the Roman historical tradition (Livy, in short).[47] In a rather similar way, fables straddle the elementary school and the poetry of Horace.[48] When Phaedrus explains that the fable was devised under the necessity of finding a way for slave to communicate frankly but safely with slave, that is, alas, no more than a rather pretty 'aetiological' invention; some sort of explanation ('aetion') of how fables began to be told that takes into account the great Greek fabulist Aesop's origins as a slave:[49] no evidence, then, for a special class of 'slave literature'[50] but yet another literary form enjoyed at Rome at all levels.

7

Hypocrisy and evidence: the case of Cicero

In the end, there is no alternative: we must face up to Cicero's evidence and the many problems it poses: its mass is vast and complex and it reveals profound inconsistencies of outlook. Cicero has been called liar, hypocrite, and worse,[1] but here it will be enough to bear clearly in mind the subject matter, the genre and the original public of the various texts cited. 'Inconstancy of judgement' may in the end do as well as 'hypocrisy'. A handful of less contentious instances may help clarify the weakness, for that it is indeed present and a weakness is hardly deniable:

Thus Cicero can pretend that he is ignorant of the most elementary details of the history of theatre and art,[2] to play up to a dully brutish chauvinism (call it haughty isolationism) never quite absent from the armoury of traditionalist Roman prejudice. He can feign ignorance of the theatre, can lament its triviality or unreality, its falsehoods (or immorality, in the case of comedy), almost in the manner of Cato (or Plato),[3] and can at the same time express a real, genuine admiration for a handful of the very best Greek actors, not merely as artists but as models for the Roman orator to imitate.[4] Naturally, in another vein, he is peculiarly well informed on ample stretches of theatrical history, comic and tragic, Greek and Roman.[5] The *plebs*, therefore, are unsurprisingly both 'filthy scum' and the like[6] and, from the same pen, the solid, respectable backbone of the *res publica*.[7] Thus we find a similar degree of consistency when we look at Cicero's observations upon the mental capacities of his popular audience.

In the speech in defence of Murena on a charge of bribery, before a *quaestio de ambitu*, Cicero is concerned to flatter the intelligence of his (equestrian) jury and purrs sententiously: 'not a speech I have to make before an inexperienced multitude or in some assembly of rustics, I shall argue rather more freely about those liberal studies which you and I know, and like'.[8] Unfortunately he then returns, in a serious philosophical discussion (*Fin.* 4.74) with the younger Cato, who had prosecuted Murena, to his earlier words and dismisses the Murena jury precisely as inexperienced, *imperiti*; he protests that he even had to make some allowance for the 'gallery'.[9] Now, though, he heaves a sigh of relief; 'time for finer (*subtilius*) discussion'. But Cicero always writes for the moment and in the *De finibus* affects to charm his Stoic interlocutor with a call to get down now to the *real* business of philosophy. Flattery of his audience (the real jury in court, Cato in an imaginary dialogue) was of course an elementary technique,[10] but there is also evidence to suggest that the airy dismissal of his earlier attempt at popularisation is not quite to be taken as Cicero's last word on the subject. Indeed, again in the *De Finibus* (5.52), an interlocutor, M. Pupius Piso Calpurnianus, takes up the problem of the appeal of useless information (such as minor details about famous men): 'and what about men of the lowest fortune, with no hope of active public life,

7. Hypocrisy and evidence: the case of Cicero

workmen, in short, who take pleasure in history?'.[11] No flattery of the audience there! Nor indeed does Cicero's testimony stand alone, for in his dedication to the emperor Titus, the elder Pliny puts a hypothetical question: what if the emperor had been just a reader of the vast *Natural History*, not a dedicatee? In that case he could have said 'but why does Your Majesty read *that*? Written for the *humili vulgo*, the common mob, for the crowd of farmers and workmen (*agricolarum, opificum turbae*) ...'.[12] To be sure, Thucydides was not suitable reading for men in the market, workmen, artisans, but because he was difficult, not because history was boring or uncongenial.[13] There were other, easier ways of learning history: as we shall see (pp. 87, 90ff.), art, oratory and the theatre taught a fair bit. Even in the country, there was no profound lack of intellectual curiosity: I don't mean just the existence of farming manuals,[14] enough to suggest a real public, but we need also to remember the neglected evidence we have for a taste for old moral saws and fairy-stories in the country[15] and the way the younger Pliny talks about rustic petitions and graffiti, or about their historical reminiscences.[16]

But let us return to Cicero: his remarks on the rhythmical ear of the public at *contiones*, mass meetings (p. 87) do not occur in contexts where we need beware of his insidious and deceitful techniques of flattery. He has seen them *exclamare*, cry out *cum apte verba cecidissent*, when the words run off properly; when, that is, the phrase concludes with a melodious metrical clausula. They sense it too when anything 'stumbles', *claudicat*, in a speech.[17] And that instinctive ear is ever-present in the theatre too: a syllable too few, or too many in a line and *theatra tota exclamant*, the whole audience cries out, not because they are experts in metre or rhythm, but because nature *gave them ears*.[18] Almost more significant, Cicero wonders how it is that the lawyer's words are often less clear than the client's would be, if he could expound his case, 'for those who bring us their cases, so inform us, for the most part, that you could not wish for a clearer exposition'.[19]

Cicero never of course denies the *plebs* their love for *ludi* and banquets;[20] on the other hand, though, he is fully aware of the collective abilities of a plebeian audience, in theatre or assembly: before such an audience, the skilled orator shall keep a good rhythm, avoid artificiality and keep off anything Greek.[21] But this sensible limitation is not part of a consistent position: when Cicero turns to philosophy, the *plebs* have lost even their function as intelligent hearers[22] and since they are altogether extraneous to the topic in hand his pen seems to distil intellectual contempt:[23] the *imperiti*, the inexpert, or profane, are also called variously *indocti* (unlearned), *stulti* (simply, 'stupid') or *insipientes* ('unwise', 'foolish'). From more temperate texts, we learn that there was at Rome and in Italy some modest popular interest in philosophy (p. 54f.), but Cicero in philosophical garb operates a threefold division, whose literary origins go back at least to the satirist Lucilius.[24] Far away, down at the bottom end, are of course the *stulti*; at the top, Cicero, naturally, and other cultivated men of reason; somewhere in between, the *mediocriter docti*, or 'passably informed'. The terminology Cicero uses varies naturally with the audience he addresses; for details, see Appendix A at the end of this chapter, p. 93f. The condemnation of the common man as 'stupid' is comprehensible in a philosophizing context,

7. Hypocrisy and evidence: the case of Cicero

and does not fully or correctly represent Cicero's considered opinion in the real world.

We have already seen how the theatre at Rome fulfilled (though this was no part of the reason for its existence) something of an educational role (p. 54ff.).[25] Popular assemblies could exercise much the same function: a full-blown speech to a *contio* (to which I come in a moment) offered the public not only a pleasant sense, perhaps even not altogether illusory, of being involved at first hand in the affairs of the republic, but could also offer, via *narrationes*, narratives of events, and *exempla*, the historical examples so beloved of Roman orators,[26] a surprising bulk of information about both geography[27] and history. In mind, naturally, are Cicero's eight[28] surviving speeches to a public meeting, plus the curious case of the speech *In defence of Gaius Rabirius, accused of treason*, delivered before the *comitia centuriata*, thirty-six years after the events which gave rise to the charge.[29]

To address 'the Roman people', at a *contio*,[30] from the *Rostra*,[31] in the heart of the Forum, must have been a remarkable challenge for the orator. There were no limits, whether by law or by usage, upon who could come; no limits therefore to the number or to the composition of the crowd;[32] barracking (and worse) was, predictably, common and not all speakers reached their conclusions quite as planned.[33] Audibility was a challenge to the speaker, for the space was not purpose-made to help him, or his hearers; indeed we really do not quite know how many citizens regularly came to *contiones*, or could hear the speeches when they did.[34] Nor were speeches the only activity of a *contio* in the Forum, where a tribune could interrogate a magistrate in public and where a (well-managed) crowd could take part in thunderous dialogue with a skilled demagogue.[35] Here the speaker was wholly at centre-stage (a striking, and ancient, metaphor),[36] could display how well his voice was trained[37] and could exercise his mastery of the quite distinct rhetorical skills[38] that the occasion and the audience required. The excellent study of Cicero's sense of place now available[39] does not distinguish the *contiones*; here, though, I concentrate on the historical references in Cicero's *contiones* and 'history' is divided roughly into three categories.

To start with recent events, 'in your memory and your fathers" as Cicero puts it:[40] to them, the orator could allude with a minimum of explanation.[41] (The defence of Rabirius (p. 87) is by comparison, an oddity: apart from the lacunae in our text of the *narratio*, the events narrated belong neither to the personal experience nor to the collective memory of the *comitia centuriata*[42] and therefore require an unusual degree of full explanation.)[43]

When Cicero refers to events between the beginning of the Second Punic War and, let us say, 100 BC, he recognises that a modest degree of detail is called for.[44]

But the large and rather miscellaneous category of events that we need to examine rather fully (for Rome still lacks a Rosalind Thomas) is what we might want to define as the historical part of a *contio*'s collective social memory, that patrimony of 'facts'[45] (not quite facts as a serious historian would understand them, mind) which an orator could presuppose and to which he could allude with a minimum of explanation. Inevitably, I shall offer some hypotheses[46] to explain the origins and transmission of parts at least of this body of memory; unfortunately research upon oral history and

7. Hypocrisy and evidence: the case of Cicero

transmission at Rome has concentrated upon a far earlier period[47] and upon certain conduits of transmission (e.g. 'banqueting songs') which we have seen (p. 33) are unlikely to yield fruitful results. Here, mindful of Rosalind Thomas' work on the Attic orators, I depend on the evidence of Cicero's surviving *contiones*: we might begin by considering the sort of historical information a Roman might acquire by assiduous attendance (their regular work, that is, permitting)[48] at assemblies and trials. We are much helped by Cicero's marked tendency (and I do not suppose his fellows in senate, courtrooms and assemblies will have been significantly different) to turn over and again to certain favourite episodes and personages (see n. 26). Thus, after his own return from exile, Cicero refers repeatedly to the analogous returns of P. Popilius Laenas, Marius and Quintus Caecilius Metellus Numidicus,[49] as to the exile of Opimius, and the full list is twice present in the version delivered at the *contio* (see n. 49). We have already glimpsed a couple of lists of famous second-century figures in *contiones*, and here *Leg. agr.* 2.64 is specially suggestive: *Luscinos, Calatinos, Acidinos*, followed shortly by *Catones, Phili, Laelii*. The plurals suggest 'people like Luscinus, etc.', with a hint that these exemplary figures bear the same names (i.e. come from the same families)[50] and again we discover that the names from the *contio* are closely paralleled in speeches to more elevated audiences;[51] Luscinus is the more familiar Fabricius, Acidinus, the more familiar A. Atilius, and that is to say that Cicero, talking to a *contio*, can use a rarer form of both names *not* used in his other speeches. About Acidinus, a singular anecdote was told (Cic. *De or.* 2.260) and we might consider whether anecdote and storytelling could have contributed to the transmission of historical details (cf. p. 110ff.). As for the second trio, the first and third names are very familiar,[52] while L. Furius Philus is absent from other oratorical lists of *exempla* but appears thus in the philosophical works.[53] This almost random enquiry does suggest strongly either that Cicero did not care whether his *contio* followed him or not (unlikely!) or that a good part of his audience was solidly familiar (most of them, that is, most of the time) with the ample canon of historical, exemplary names, presumably from assiduous attendance in the Forum. A similar conclusion may well hold good for the laws of C. Gracchus and for the revolt of Fregellae (see Appendix B(A) at the end of this chapter, p. 94): the latter is found in a list of *exempla* at *Rhet. Her.* (pre-Ciceronian) 4.37, the former appears in such lists likewise, at *Sest.* 103, *Phil.* 1.18.

These *exempla* (men and episodes alike) may seem unmemorable when reduced to mere names; less so when the lists are expanded into short stories and much less so when the stories/heroes are known to have been commemorated in some quite different medium. It would be most welcome to be able to invoke historical tragedy (cf. p. 160, n. 3), but on the little evidence we have, that is not a solidly demonstrable link. Surprisingly, however, it is works of art and even inscriptions visible in the city's public places that may come to our rescue.[54] This is not the moment to enter into the debate(s) on how easily understood the works of art exposed to view actually were to the man in the street (and in general, on the relationship of art and public), on the need for explanatory texts and labels and their legibility, lack, or otherwise, on the efficacy of art as propaganda and on just what the public of art-in-the-

7. Hypocrisy and evidence: the case of Cicero

street was.⁵⁵ In good measure, moreover, this public collection of art was an anthology of two centuries of varied booty, an ever-present consequence of conquest.⁵⁶ Not everything in this accidental museum was, however, easily understood. Thus Lucius Hostilius Mancinus, a hero of the siege of Carthage in 148-7 BC, had exposed in the Forum a fresco representing the city and the Roman assaults; the admiral stood there in person (*ipse adsistens*) to explain the details (*singula enarrando*) to the spectators (*populo spectanti*), and secured thereby a consulate in 145.⁵⁷ In his four triumphs, Julius Caesar preferred to attach no names to the representations of his victories, hoping thereby to reduce the awkwardness of a long series of battles fought, and won, against fellow-citizens,⁵⁸ while Ovid's famous scene of viewing a triumphal procession in the company of an impressionable young woman (p. 109) presupposes that either she *and* the young man are short-sighted or they are not all properly labelled.⁵⁹ In a *contio*, Cicero speaks of a statue – visible to the orator and to his public – of Quintus Tremulus, conqueror of the Hernici, before the temple of Castor.⁶⁰ More important are the three cases there seem to be (and more may emerge from further studies of the material) of links between historical references in *contiones* and art on show. First, the luxury of Capua which corrupted Hannibal and his army;⁶¹ this was so familiar as to be proverbial⁶² – and why should proverbs not have helped transmit some scraps of historical information? – but must also have been known from the substantial booty brought home, some part of which could reasonably be supposed to have survived, on view, with some sort of identification.⁶³ In the same speech (*Leg. Man.* 90), Cicero, in a list of famous wars against Kings Philip, Antiochus, Perseus, Mithridates ..., inserts the war against Pseudo-Philip (149-8 BC), specially known at Rome on account of the *Porticus Metelli*,[64] with no inscription from the dedicator, but a rich depository of Macedonian statuary. We return, lastly, to ch. 64, *Luscinos, Calatinos, Acidinos*, who belonged, we have just seen (n. 51) to the stock, familiar lists of exemplary figures. But Fabricius Luscinus was also commemorated by a statue set up at the expense of the city of Thurii, once saved by him, in 282 BC.[65]

We may also wonder whether prominent commemorative inscriptions have some place in this argument. Large epigraphic capitals, after all, would be prodigiously useful as texts to teach reading to children in the city's public places.[66]

This is not the moment to list all the epigraphic references we have (and may once have had) to all the personages named in Cicero's *contiones*, and I limit myself to two further interesting and closely related cases from *Leg. agr.* 2: the defeat of Aristonicus (ch. 90), celebrated with a triumph, and thus commemorated in inscriptions (over and above the *Fasti Triumphales*) in honour of Manius Aquilius (consul, 129). The case of his son (ch. 83) is yet more singular: he won not a triumph, but an *ovatio* after the Servile War of 101-99 (and so there may have been some visible commemorative inscription) and was also honoured by a statue set up by the state, as normally happened in the case of a death which had taken place *iniuria*, in breach of international law, as Cicero explains to us, indeed in the course of another *contio*.[67] We are no nearer knowing exactly how Cicero's public coped with all the history he tossed at them, but the fact of his doing so, so much and so often, requires us to offer some account of how his public was intellectually able to handle so much historical

7. Hypocrisy and evidence: the case of Cicero

allusion, not least when we clearly cannot assume that that public went home nightly to read Cato's *Origines*.

Appendix A. Cicero's terminology

[P indicates philosophical texts]

barbari, 'savage, barbarian', used of *operarii*, workmen, individually and collectively (*Tusc. Disp.* 5.104 (P)).

mediocriter docti, 'half-educated': even they can follow what the Epicurean populariticians profess, *Tusc. Disp.* 2.7 (P). Compare *Acad.* 1.5 (P), Rawson (1985), 49, n. 49. See too (P) *Fin.* 3.3, *Leg.* 3.14 *mediocriter docti* who are great men in the state.

insipientes, 'foolish': *Tusc. Disp.* 2.63 (P), the *vulgus*, or crowd, of the *i*.

stulti, 'stupid': do not appear a *sapiens* among them (below, n. 21): we are in a context of rhetorical precepts. Note the similar use of *agrestis*, 'rustic', (P) *Parad. Stoic.* 33, *Rep.* 1.23.

indocti, 'unlearned': does not want to write what the *indocti* could not read, (P) *Acad.* 1.4 (cf. *Off.* 1.1). (P) *Fin.* 1.1: even those not really unlearned, *non admodum indocti* have no taste for philosophy; *ib.* 72, to the *indocti*, what they learned in youth is enough for the rest of their lives. *Nat. Deor.* 1.55 (P), the opinions of the *indocti* a target. At *Pis.* 68 *non apud indoctos loquor* is typical (p. 84) flattery of his audience.

imperiti, 'inexpert'. We recall (cf. p. 84) the philosopher's view of the non-competent audience of *Pro Murena, Fin.* 4.74; cf. (P) *ib.* 2.74, *Off.* 1.65, 3.15; compare, in oratory, the non-specialist audience, *De orat.* 3.195. The *imperiti* have opinions, however, *Mil.* 62, and express them (*sermones, Clu.*

5; contrasted, the wits of the competent, *ingenia prudentium*), noisily *clamore multitudinis imperitae*, *Lig.* 3. Familiar language in the speeches, indeed (*Flacc.* 2, 97, *Dom.* 4, 54, *Phil.* 2, 116: Caesar sweetened, *delenierat* the *multitudinem imperitam*; cf. *ib.* 12.28 soldiers an *imperita multitudo*). The *ignara multitudo* (*rerum omnium rudes*, bereft of everything, he continues) of *Flacc.* 16 refers to the unbridled *libertas* of a Greek assembly, seated, against Roman usage (cf. Millar 1998, 221). The *imperiti* easily stirred, *Verr.* 2.1.151, 5.163. When, therefore, Cic. was not speaking to a popular audience, he referred (fairly enough, on any argument) to the crowd's lack of experience of public affairs (cf. Hellegouarc'h, 514).

Appendix B. Cicero's exempla

(A) Cf. in particular *Leg. agr.* 2.51 (Scipio and the territory of Carthage; a brief explanation offered; cf. *Leg. Man.* 60), 82 (P. Lentulus, cos. 162; cf. *MRR* 1, 442. Cic. explains briefly), 90 (revolt of Fregellae; a rhetorical sequence: cf. *Rhet. Her.* 4.22,37), 64 (the elder Cato, C. Laelius, L. Furius Philus as distinguished Romans; cf. Cic. *Amic.* 21), *Phil.* 6.10 (Scipio Africanus and (alas, the name is lost!) as distinguished figures), *Rab. Perd.* 12-15 (laws of C. Gracchus), *Phil.* 6.4 (envoys sent to Hannibal to discourage him from the siege of Saguntum; now slightly problematic: see *MRR* s.v. 219 BC). Note *Leg. agr.* 2.50ff., royal lands which have passed to Rome, *Leg. Man.* 55 history of Roman seapower.

(B) Cf. for example Cic. *Leg. Man.* 30 (Spartacus), 28-30 (first campaigns of Pompey), *Post red. ad Quir.* 7 (Marius' return from exile; cf. 19, 20), *Cat.* 3.24, *Leg. agr.* 3.5-8 (some

7. Hypocrisy and evidence: the case of Cicero

knowledge of the history of Marius and Sulla is presupposed; the speech is likewise a *contio*), *Cat.* 3.9 (destruction of the Capitol in 83 BC), *Leg. agr.* 2.90 (social war), *ib.* 62 (events of 91 BC), *Leg. Man.* 8 (triumphs after the war against Mithridates). The kidnapping of a son of the orator M. Antonius by pirates mentioned, without identification, *Leg. Man.* 33.

8

Implications

This book was not written to solve a problem or close a discussion: it has suggested some new evidence, some new authors to consider, and a new 'line'. If some of the results are largely acceptable, then there is a lot of new work to be done, with, however, some degree of caution. Oral history and the oral transmission of poetry, myths and legends carry a unique attraction: they exist, solidly and beyond any doubt; the information they yield is unchallengeably real, and yet by comparison with the boring, conventional written record, they are impalpable, fleeting, primitive, remote. There were no anthropologists with tape-recorders at Roman banquets, and for two centuries[1] scholars have in their imaginations hidden behind the arras to try to reconstruct what might have been heard. The result is a nexus of long-running controversies: many of them, on any dispassionate view, ought to be regarded as settled, yet they will not lie down and die. My position is paradoxical: I have just argued at length for a rich popular culture, in many respects oral in character, at Rome, and yet the arguments for an oral transmission or diffusion of stories from history, myth, or legend have not hitherto convinced me. That is because the evidence is solidly against the hypothesis of such transmission.[2] This sounds very tiresome: of course I

8. Implications

can see that historical tragedies (*fabulae praetextae*),[3] banqueting songs,[4] ritual laments,[5] travelling storytellers[6] and the like *could* so easily have transmitted all manner of material from the dim and distant Roman past, just as they have done in many other cultures. We can be pretty sure that art, speeches, and rituals did indeed do just that. And that indeed may be just the point: we have as it is several demonstrably effective channels of transmission and there seems to be no great need to construct new hypotheses of alternative means of transmission which are not only unprovable but frankly unnecessary.

For a Roman author, to cite an oral source was not just a simple act of citing a real oral source, but was rather the studied display of a complex, traditional literary mannerism, which had been much in vogue since Callimachus' time (early/mid-third century BC), and was not limited to prose.[7] That, alas, means that we are not free to make deductions from those many passages in which (for example) Ovid cites an apparent conversation with A or B: such 'inventions' must be entirely credible, but need never be precise and authoritative whether in 'scenery' or in actual content.[8] Roman banqueting-songs were already literary fossils when Varro (*c.* 50 BC), even when Cato (early/mid-second century BC) wrote about them: subject the very little we are told to proper, careful analysis and it looks very much as though no actual songs had survived even to Cato's time and very little detailed information was still preserved about them. What Cato tells us about the songs' content ('the praises and brave deeds of famous men')[9] does not allow us to infer that the content could also have been mythological or legendary. There remains a nasty and inescapable suspicion: that what we are told about these *carmina convivalia* is not real information about them but rather, as I have argued at length (n. 4), a learned borrowing, just like virtually everything else we are told about archaic Latin literature, from learned Hellenistic writing about archaic Greece, and in this case in particular from the scholarly tradition about Greek banqueting-songs.[10] Once this suspicion is established as *prima facie* likely or reasonable, what we are told about the *carmina convivalia* is reduced, alas, to very limited value. There seems to be no point in reconstructing the *carmina* by comparison with what we are told was archaic Greek usage, when our evidence for their very existence turns out to be in all probability no more than a rough reworking of Aristotle and Dicaearchus on Greek symposium-songs. If my nasty suspicion can be laid to rest by further patient analysis of the evidence, then serious discussion might start all over again.

The transmission of myth and legend at Rome has attracted a great deal of attention,[11] but no clear and certain trace of its oral transmission has been found, nor even any form of ritual or entertainment (outside, naturally, the theatre) specially well-suited to such transmission, which, I fear, must remain a delightful and inviting hypothesis, just as it was when first advanced in 1812. What changes, fascinatingly, is the readiness of scholars to listen to such siren songs and to repeat them as though they were the results of real, solid research. That leaves us with (cf. p. 57) the *circulator*, the man who entertains a *circulus*, or little crowd gathered round him. Under Trajan, Dio Chrysostom (20.10) writes of going to the Circus Maximus and seeing a man playing the flute, another dancing, another performing a trick (*thauma*), another reading a poem, another singing, another relating a story (*historian*) or myth

8. Implications

(*mython*), not explicitly a *circulator*, but, to be honest, near enough.[12] The date is significant, for Trajan's reign was no longer a time at which Rome had any sort of active mythology; occasional scholars may have tinkered with old received material and embroidered some new detail, but readers of Juvenal and Tacitus were not about to relish a lurid, ample reconstruction of the story of the kings of Alba. The storyteller of the Circus Maximus had the whole repertory of classical myth at his disposal, perhaps even the *Odyssey*, retold in Latin for the Greekless, but that does not make him a key figure at Rome in the oral transmission of a mythology still fresh and living.[13] However, even without its own oral myths, the popular culture so far outlined seems for now rich and varied enough.

At that point, though the Roman *plebs* may not yet quite have reacquired intellectual respectability, the beginnings of a case have been offered to suggest that Volteius Mena and his peers really could look some distance beyond booze and bawdy. The publication of this argument may seem to be timed to catch a fashionable wind, now that the traditional view[13] of the *plebs* as helpless victim of patrician manipulation no longer rules unchallenged among historians of the late republic. When I first wrote of Roman popular culture, it was indeed in the much more limited and friendly context of the freedmen in Petronius' *Cena Trimalchionis*;[14] now the man in the Roman street is regaining a significant political role, just at a time when the world of his pleasures, interests and leisure activities is being revealed as rich and varied.[15] This coincidence, naturally, is not merely fortuitous. Active visitors to the theatre and to *contiones* (p. 87) in the Forum, men quick over their sums at the backgammon board, and quick too in informed repartee[16] are of course, naturally, inevitably more willing and more able to take that more active and committed part in public life – beyond, that is, mere abuse, shoving and half-bricks[17] – which Prof. Millar and his allies attribute to them.

There has been another political sub-text in these pages, of which I would like to say a little more in conclusion, a variation upon Trevelyan's famous remark 'if the French *noblesse* had been capable of playing cricket with their peasants, their chateaux would never have been burnt'.[18] It did seem as though our ill-assorted travellers in their inn on the coast of Puglia (p. 77f.) will have known how to pass their time until the wind changed.[19] Had Volteius Mena (but was he a real historical character? We do not know!) been able to meet Augustus they could agreeably have swapped good stories about the theatre, for a start. The *princeps* was no intellectual.[20] That very aristocracy which, on the traditional view of republican politics, cynically manipulated the *plebs* to its own ends, actually shared, as we have learned, many of the pastimes and pleasures of that very *plebs*.

The concept of a common fund of pleasures shared at all levels of society is very comforting:[21] it warms our innate sense of democracy and seems to promise lasting, widely-based security. 'Shared pleasures', however, conceal numerous moments of uncomfortable reality: the myth of cricket as a sport for all conceals the reluctance of the wealthy amateur to bowl.[22] The story of Volteius Mena and Marcius Philippus, indeed, is all about, *inter alia*, the deep problems inherent in cross-caste social relations. But at Rome some common pleasures (theatre, games in the *Campus Martius*, gaming) do seem to have existed, however little and uncomfortably shared in

8. Implications

reality. The Romans failed to invent cricket, but, to return to Trevelyan, we might ask whether it was in part at least because of long hot days watching revivals of Pacuvius and Terence together (not to mention gladiators and chariot-races) that a howling mob did not storm the Capitol on 14 July 89 BC.[23]

Appendix 1

The legionary as his own historian[1]

In memory of Norman Austin,
militis minime gloriosi[2]

Outside the Colosseum, in English museums and even, I gather, tramping from Munich to Italy, you are liable to meet enthusiasts dressed in full Roman armour. The exquisitely painful boot-nail which lands on your toe at Juvenal 3.248 (compare 16.24) belongs specifically to a *miles* (who is therefore presumably uniformed). Could you, though, spot a Roman veteran? The hunt for his distinguishing features (and if some of my evidence applies primarily to a soldier out of uniform, it will be cited none the less) was productive and satisfying, as might actually have been predicted, given the deeply-rooted links in Greco-Roman thinking (consider Homer's Thersites, or Theophrastus' *Characters*) between appearance or manners and character or activity.[3] So Seneca discusses the emotions (symptoms, we might say) which are preliminary to full-blown passions and cites the case of the *militaris uir* [warrior], in the midst of peace and wearing his toga: he pricks up his ears at the sound of a trumpet, just as the clank of arms stirs the old army horse (*Ira* 2.2.6). Suetonius, notoriously, owes much to the conventions of ancient

Appendix 1

physiological writing[4] and says that Vespasian was *statura ... quadrata, compactis firmisque membris* [of square build, with solid, muscular limbs] (*Vesp.* 20.1): predictably, for he came of solid centurion stock. But the typical soldier did not just look like Vespasian, and detail, satiric to be sure, but also specific, abounds: they had hairy nostrils, short back and sides, wide shoulders, heavy muscular development, bulging calves, varicose veins from too much marching; they did not pluck their leg hair and they were perceptibly careless of personal hygiene.[5] Even Ennius (*Ann.* 249Sk.) refers to the *miles* as *horridus*: the word is primarily tactile (cf. my note on *Aeneid* 7.746), though often more emotive than a mere 'bristly'. Horace's unloved schoolfellows at Venusia were 'hulking boys born of hulking centurions';[6] Persius went one better (5.190) and calls centurions *ingentes*, vast; they were[7] after all chosen for their strength. Predictably, they were quarrelsome, and Cicero cites the centurion and *signifer* [standard-bearer] as typical of those who cannot resort to reason and turn therefore to anger;[8] it was you that apologised when one crushed your toe. You also knew a soldier by the way he talked, that is, by the distinctive *sermo campestris*, field idiom.[9] Perhaps also by the bars he frequented.[10] Not to mention his scars: Manlius Capitolinus, who 'saved the Capitol' from the Gauls' assault in 390 BC, is said to have had twenty-three.[11] The one-eyed man was very likely to have been an old soldier; Caesar talks of four centurions in a single cohort who lost eyes at the siege of Dyrrhachium.[12] There were men (*murci*) who cut their thumbs off to avoid further service, but Catiline's grandfather fought left-handed, having lost his right hand in battle and some such story must underly the *cognomen* Mancinus in the

The legionary as his own historian

Gens Hostilia.[13] There may of course have been exceptions, like the soldier in civilian dress who sits down next to you in Rome and begins to talk ill of the emperor.[14]

An ugly mob, to judge from hostile sources! Other have charted in alarming detail the recruitment of criminals into the army, the notorious role of the soldier as thief and bully and the easy passage thereafter from 'soldier' to full-time bandit,[15] but the profound and ultimately catastrophic disenchantment felt by civilians towards the army[16] is a development only foreshadowed by the late republican and early imperial sources on which this book largely rests. We are now warned (justifiably enough) about the dangers of using the model of the soldier in modern society when writing about the Roman army,[17] but rigorously correct method can blind the student of military behaviour to invaluable clues. Ramsay MacMullen's use of recent studies of unit solidarity in his engrossing 'The legion as a society'[18] points the way to a more constructive use of parallel material. I confess willingly to a passable collection of military and naval history books and to relishing good (ex-)service talk;[19] if in the end this paper offers an explanation for just where an odd and neglected collection of bits of evidence may lead us, it is perhaps just *because* for almost fifty years I have actively listened to, and read, a considerable body of just this kind of anecdotage!

Areas of contact between soldier and civilian during the peaceful years of the early empire need to be measured judiciously: the violence and destruction under the second triumvirate and in 69 AD was geographically limited[20] and that limitation in turn may have conditioned the diffusion and survival in Italy of a collective memory of the *impius miles*'

Appendix 1

[cruel soldier's] ravages and brutality. Otherwise, we might think that only praetorians (and soldiers of the urban cohorts) were visible in Rome;[21] elsewhere in Italy they seem to have been a particularly rare sight (Nippel (n. 21), 91), but[22] individually were figures of real moment in their towns of origin. However, this paper is not concerned with Italy alone, for though it is Rome where the satirists' caricature of the warrior is located, the impact of the soldier as storyteller is essentially ubiquitous: the 'world of the Golden Ass' is formally located in Central and Northern Greece (Millar (n. 16), 64ff.), yet its author was a North African and in some ways the sociohistorical validity of Apuleius' novel is empire-wide (cf. Millar, 66). Nor should we forget that maps which illustrate the distribution of the legions across the empire perforce obscure an army in continuous movement: the experts, like tunnel-engineers, are a rather special case[23] and we notice that Nonius Datus[24] travelled *cum meis* [with escort], little good though they did him in the face of Mauretanian bandits. On imperial bodyguards we are amply informed (Millar (1977), 61ff.), but the reality of empire-wide endemic banditry[25] will have meant that officers promoted and transferred, special equipment and supplies, and communications of major importance all required proper escorts.[26] Along the great highways of the empire, I suspect that the inns were full of officials, officers and small bodies of soldiers, making the best of long journeys. *Militantibus ex omnibus prouincis* [men on duty from all provinces] as the *legatus pro praetore* [praetor's legate] of Pisidia wrote, *c.* AD 15,[27] in his regulations for the requisition of transport.

There was, too, regular leave for soldiers: not just blank

The legionary as his own historian

spaces on their duty rosters, but actual leave to go home, though the individual soldier was sometimes driven sometimes to ask an oracle to know when it was due![28] Before the Marian reforms, military service had not, except in times of crisis, been continuous[29] and *hiberna*, the winter quarters of the Roman army,[30] was one of the first neuter plural nouns we once learned. There was time for fighting, and time for talking, in the context of the serving soldier's daily routine, on which, thanks to the late R. W. Davies' fascinating work (n. 28) we are now solidly well-informed. Drill and bull,[31] not to mention heavy manual labour in aid of the civil administration[32] did not (cf. n. 28) entirely fill the soldier's day. The Roman army, inevitably as bored as any other regular army outside its rare moments of appalling activity[33] did have time to drink, on a truly imperial scale,[34] both wine and beer, as the centurion Mascius has immortalised in his appeal to Cerealis, prefect of the Ninth Cohort of Batavians, *ceruesam commilitones non habunt* [not a rare mis-spelling] *quam rogo iubeas mitti* [the lads have no beer; please give orders for sending same];[35] the bars in the *canabae* [shanty-towns][36] round the regular camps were necessarily the hothouses that bred the military anecdote.

The legions were quintessential closed societies and it is no idle fancy of mine to suggest that they had a 'culture' of their own: certainly slang, humour and even grammar were distinctive and recognisable.[37] The solidarity which binds together a unit's soldiers and veterans is not just an inference from modern times, but rests on epigraphic evidence[38] and is the natural product of the legionaries' tendency to retire *together*, to unit-based colonies or areas, where they enjoyed relative

Appendix 1

wealth, status, privileges and their own *collegia*, clubs or associations.[39] The case of the veterans of Octavian's Eleventh Legion is decisive: they settled at Ateste, modern Este, south of Padua, and on their tombstones specified that they were precisely and specifically *Actiaci*, veterans of Actium; that they celebrated the battle's anniversary, 2 September, with riotous solemnity, rather, of course, as Australians and New Zealanders still celebrate Anzac Day, seems overwhelmingly likely.[40] Denis Feeney reminds me of Ovid's eminently credible conversation with a retired military tribune at the theatre (*Fasti* 4.377ff.): a proud (and eloquent) veteran of Thapsus, on 6 April, Thapsus Day, naturally. Until AD 20, or 30, such talk of Actium will have been common currency.

The veteran's loyalties and distinguished service were also visible in other ways:[41] the *corona ciuica*, the crown won for saving the life of a fellow-citizen [*ciuis*] in battle, entitled its holder to wear special robes at festivals (Polybius 6.39.9) and when such a hero – entitled to wear his crown for the rest of his life – went to the *ludi* [games, theatre], crowned, clearly (cf. Livy 10.47.3), even the senators rose to him, and he was entitled to sit next to them; usefully, but less showily, he was also exempted from civic duties, as were his father and grandfather (Pliny *Nat.* 16.13). It matters not at all if the story told at Livy 3.58.8 is anachronistic or unhistorical, so long as we recognise that the image of a veteran going to court to give evidence wearing twenty-seven campaign medals and eight special awards (*extra ordinem donatus*) was in no way false to regular usage.

Old warriors will have been specially prominent, too, on certain occasions: not just the anniversaries of their victories,

The legionary as his own historian

as I have suggested, but also the re-enactments of great naval battles, unsurprisingly including Actium (Hor. *Epist.* 1.18.61f.: in private) and variously attested from Caesar to Titus.[42] Their reaction to displays of booty,[43] to trophies, monuments, reliefs[44] and processions we can, I suggest, extrapolate from Ovid's famous scene of the young seducer impressing his target at the triumph anticipated on Gaius' return from the East: the girl will ask the names of the kings, the places, the mountains, the river. Answer the lot, advises the poet (and add a bit). Get them right, if you can; if you don't know, make them sound good, *ut bene nota/ apta tamen* [as though you knew them; at any rate plausible] (*AA* 1.222, 228). But just think of the actual veteran in all his glory: he had doubtless been there and doubtless kept talking hours after the procession ended. The hairy thugs with whom we began are after all extraordinarily important – whether serving or retired – as the civilian's closest link with battles, history, empire, enemies, frontiers, the edges of the known world.

Soldiers' talk and legionary slang are distinct but not jealously protected and it is easy to see how they overflow into common speech, as they had done at Athens:[45] in Plautus' texts, in proverbs of military content, or in the use of military metaphors in erotic talk.[46] The yarns told by fighting men are very old: sea stories began with Odysseus (or Noah) and army anecdotes with Nestor. Service talk and the literary representation of the fighting man (or veteran) have, in general, a long literary history, studied only in part:[47] heroic and aristocratic, widely diffused in the age of citizen armies, then transmuted again in the day of the Hellenistic mercenary (and his heirs in Roman comedy). The development of the *miles*

Appendix 1

gloriosus [boastful soldier] is a particular comic-satiric variant of the poetic/theatrical soldier; he swaggers on stage in Aristophanes (where military service has acquired, as in the case of Creon, political importance) and is still swaggering nearly three centuries later. But the *gloriosi* are a distraction.[48] I am more interested in the old men who talked to Herodotus of their wars,[49] in the question posed by Xenophanes in a symposium-song 'How old were you when the Mede came?',[50] in the chronological confusion into which the old men in *Wasps* and *Lysistrata* fall, as old soldiers will do,[51] in the wonderful fancy of exotic lands rendered yet stranger that we find in a fragment of Antiphanes – of the king of Cyprus fanned by his doves over dinner,[52] and last, but by no means least, of Theophrastus' late-learner who learns his drill terms from his son.[53]

Now that Richard Saller has rehabilitated the historical value of the anecdote[54] and we have learned from various distinguished scholars how hitherto neglected areas of the history of Roman society and institutions can be coaxed back into life on the basis of great scattered masses of miscellaneous and apparently trivial evidence,[55] we can look at last at the Roman military anecdote without worrying unduly about the extremely heterogeneous character of the evidence on offer. Perhaps indeed its variety suggests how widespread it was and how many more instances are hidden away out there awaiting resuscitation. For now I offer six specific pieces of evidence which do seem to suggest that legionaries were in truth enthusiastic story-tellers; it is worth adding both that Martial has centurion friends[56] and that not only biographers, but serious historians – even the notoriously fastidious Tacitus – record as worthy of interest and permanent record the frequently significant remarks and humours of the rank and file.[57] As Nicholas Purcell has remarked to me, the army focuses all those upwards and downwards social contacts which we are beginning to find in Roman society at large. The specially important army story has every chance of literary immortality and many instances of the legions' oral culture have already been gathered by others, working to quite different ends.

Thus, white charlock (?), Albanian *kelkass*, Lat. *lapsana*, upon which I stumbled in E. Courtney's collection of the fragments of *uersus triumphales* [triumph-songs],[58] for Pliny had himself picked it – but as a botanical curiosity – somewhere in his vast reading. Caesar's troops, besieging Dyrrhachium, had been reduced to eating this doubtful delicacy and in his triumph they reproved him (admiringly) for having kept them on such rations. Caesar himself records his soldiers as saying that they'd rather eat the bark off the trees than give up the siege (*B. Civ.* 3.49.1). Hardships endured together (cf. MacMullen (n. 18, 1990), 231f.) and oddities of local diet are the very stuff of military anecdote (and unit solidarity), far rather than the bloody detail of combat. Sieges have just the right tempo, as do mutinies, for the generation, and recording, of the common soldier's eloquence, and it is no accident that we are so richly informed on the commissariat problems during this very siege – and the unconventional solutions that were tried out.[59]

When the future emperor Galba took over a command from Gaetulicus under Caligula, to avoid bursts of applause, he gave orders for hands to be kept under cloaks and *per castra iactatum est, disce miles militare: Galba est non Gaetulicus* [round the camp went the line 'soldier, learn to serve: it's

Appendix 1

Galba, not Gaetulicus'] (Courtney (1993), 480): the metre is that of the *carmina triumphalia* [triumph songs] but this verse may be the lonely survivor of the Roman army's heritage of song; to music they must have marched, if only to keep step and thus avoid serious injury and their marching-songs will necessarily have been a key element (the key element, indeed) in their collective memory.[60] The eagerness with which verses of the *carmina triumphalia* were preserved and cited shows that their importance was perceived rather as Aristotle grasped the crucial importance grasped the crucial importance of sympotic song.[61]

The *SHA* life of Hadrian enshrines (17.6-8) a long and delicious anecdote, whose historicity is not to my knowledge impugned and whose significance needs to be disentangled: the emperor went regularly to the public baths and one day saw (whence the fame of this *balnearis iocus* [bath-house joke]) a veteran he knew, scratching his back, and the rest of his body, against the bath-house wall. 'How so? No slave?' 'No, sir.' The veteran is given a slave and money. The day after, *plures senes* [several old men] are rubbing themselves against the wall. The emperor orders them over [*euocari*] to rub each other down in turn [*alium ab alio defricari*]. That tells us that an emperor might reasonably stop to chat in the baths with an old *commilito* [companion-at-arms], but, more important, it should be recognised as a subtle parody of weapons drill. Naturally I thought first of Kirk Douglas learning gladiatorial skills under Peter Ustinov's disenchanted eye, net against trident, trident against net, etc., but one rapidly discovers that army weapons training derives from the gladiatorial schools and that numbering off (presumably) to take turns, ones against twos and twos

The legionary as his own historian

against ones, is a regular element in that training,[62] as the hopeful but thwarted veterans will not have failed to remember.

Or take the centurion Lucilius at Tacitus *Ann.* 1.23.3 who had received, in the soldiers' jokes (*militaribus facetiis*) the sobriquet 'Gimme another', *cedo alteram*, from his way of breaking one vine-staff across a soldier's back and yelling [*clara uoce ... poscebat*] for another and yet another. Mutinies, we have seen (p. 111) are just the moment at which the soldier's voice has to be heard,[63] and Tacitus at the same time lowers his stylistic level (*cedo*) to characterise the uncouth and brutal types then promoted to centurion.

Real soldiers (and sailors) do not, I repeat, talk endlessly about their battles. It was above all, I think, Emilio Gabba who first taught us to perceive the penetration of tales of travel and largely fabulous accounts of distant lands into high literature;[64] others soon followed.[65]

Hans Aili has recently proposed a most elegant explanation[66] of the hotly disputed elks of Caesar *BG* 6.25ff.: not, he suggests, to be expelled from the text as a dotty fantasy unworthy of Caesar, but to be understood as a compromise between a literary account, one rather like the unknown source of Diodorus 3.27, and an inexpert observer's description, direct or reported, of an elk shedding its old horns. Certainly strange enough to earn the teller another cup of *posca* [vinegar and water] or *zythum* [beer] (if nothing better was to hand) in the *cannabae*. It is worth remembering that Petronius' novella of the Widow of Ephesus was told to an audience of sailors (113.1) and that Crassus' officers carried Aristides' Milesian tales with them on campaign (Plut. *Crass.* 32.4). Armies and navies have always had not only enemies,

Appendix 1

but time to kill, and audiences used to similar experiences. Though Matthew 27.35, the soldiers dicing for Christ' garments, is no more than the fulfilment of Psalm 22.18, it is perfectly in keeping with the army's passion for gaming[67] and in camp narrative will have become something like 'And do you know what I won in that game? Only a dirty shirt, soaked in blood. Had to throw it away.' And as Tennyson wrote of Ulysses, much had they seen and known: not many had sailed the North Sea with Drusus, or reached the depths of the German forests, not to mention the Yemen, Ethiopia, Fezzan, Mauretania, Armenia, and the Kingdom of Fife,[68] but some had gone, and come back to tell the tale. Not a bad way of keeping your glass filled for a few years. 'Those who have crossed seas and lands are delighted when they are asked about a place on land or some bay of the sea unknown to the multitude. They reply gladly and describe now in words, now with a stick the places, thinking it a proud boast to set before the eyes of others what they have themselves seen.' So Macrobius, in the early fifth century AD, but paraphrasing Plutarch,[69] and for that matter, perfectly in keeping with Homer. Even Nonius Datus (n. 24, above) was able to relate – at least to our certain knowledge, for his specialist experience may have left him with a far richer fund of stories – his clash with the bandits and the long struggle to re-dig a tunnel through the mountain to bring water to Saldae, Bougie, working from both ends and meeting, this time, in the middle.

So we reach Tibullus 1.10.31f.:

> Vt mihi potanti possit sua dicere facta
>   miles et in mensa pingere castra mero.

The legionary as his own historian

[So the soldier may tell me his deeds as I drink and draw his camp in the wine]. The couplet lurks in a rather limp and conventional denunciation of war and warriors: the content might also seem to lie open to a conventional attack along the lines of 'a theme so familiar that we have no idea whether such things ever really happened'. Ovid is full of lovers' messages written in the wine at dinner[70] and we are familiar with the scene of the Athenians busily drawing ambitious maps of Sicily.[71] To Penelope, Ulysses sketched the Trojan war in his wine; he was used to it, for he had already done so to Calypso, in the sand.[72] But sometimes, as we have learned,[73] commonplaces are so common precisely because they really did correspond to daily usage, and it seems by this point to have emerged that Ulysses is acting exactly as any returned veteran, by land or by sea, would naturally have done, and in sober fact often did, in taverns empire-wide, and so well that historians have often picked up the results and immortalised them.

Appendix 2

Some inscriptions

There has recently been exceptionally valuable work on the exact linguistic level of inscriptions (vulgarisms, significant errors, elements of dialect, identification of the Latin of likely second-language writers), notably by Prof. J.N. Adams (e.g. *Journ. Rom. Stud.* 89 (1999), 109-34, 'The poets of Bu Njem: language, culture and the centurionate'). Here, much more modestly, I take a handful of inscriptional texts (reproduced without the full epigraphic apparatus) on which I have already worked and try to show something of how they can all now be used as evidence for the differentiation of educational and cultural levels. Two of the five I choose are clearly not 'plebeian' in origin, but they do both show neatly enough that social elevation does not automatically correspond to cultural advantages.

(1) *Inscr. Lat. Sel.* 8393, *cum additamentis*, '*Laudatio Turiae*'.[1] The longest private inscription in Latin: the mid-Augustan funeral eulogy of an unidentified woman [the bad, old ascription 'Turia' is perfectly irrelevant]. Here, col. 2, lines 11-28. I give Wistrand's text, and – mostly – the translation on which I worked closely with him, though some of Flach's supplements do merit serious consideration.

Some inscriptions

Acerbissumum tamen in vi[ta] mihi accidisse tua vice fatebo[r reddito me iam] cive patriae beneficio et i[ud]icio apsentis Caesaris Augusti, [quom per te] de restitutione mea M. L[epi]dus conlega praesens interp[ellaretur et ad eius] pedes prostrata humi [n]on modo non adlevata sed tra[cta et servilem in] modum rapsata, livori[ibus c]orporis repleta, firmissimo [animo eum admone]res edicti Caesaris cum g[r]atulatione restitutionis me[ae auditisque verbis eti]am contumeliosis et cr[ud]elibus exceptis volneribus pa[lam ea praeferres.] ut auctor meorum peric[ul]orum notesceret. Quoi no[cuit mox ea res].

Quid hac virtute efficaciu[s], praebere Caesari clementia[e locum et cum cu]stodia spiritus mei not[a]re inportunam crudelitatem [Lepidi egregia tua] patientia?

Sed quid plura? Parcamu[s] orationi, quae debet et potest e[sse brevis, ne maxi]ma opera tractando pa[r]um digne peragamus, quom pr[o magnitudine erga me] meritorum tuorum oc[ulis] omnium praeferam titulum [vitae servatae.]

Pacato orbe terrarum, res[titut]a re publica, quieta deinde n[obis et felicia] tempora contigerunt. Fue[ru]nt optati liberi, quos aliqua[mdiu sors invi]derat. si fortuna procede[re e]sset passa sollemnis inservie[ns, quid utrique no]strum defuit?

But I must say that the bitterest thing that happened to me in my life befell me through what happened to you. When, thanks to the kindness and judgement of the absent Caesar Augustus, I had been restored to my coun-

Appendix 2

try as a citizen, thanks to you, Marcus Lepidus, his colleague, who was present, was confronted with a request concerning my recall, and you, prostrate on the ground at his feet, were not only not raised up, but were carried away and dragged off as are slaves. Covered as you were with bruises, yet your spirit was unbroken and you reminded him of Caesar's edict with its compliments upon my reinstatement and though you listened to insulting words and suffered cruel wounds, you pronounced the words of the edict in a loud voice, so that it should be known who was the cause of my perils. This matter was soon to prove harmful for him.

What could have been more effective than the virtue you showed? You gave Caesar the chance to show clemency and both to save my life and by your admirable endurance to show up Lepidus' insolent cruelty.

But why go on? Let me cut short my speech. My words should and can be brief, lest by dwelling on your great deeds I treat them unworthily. In gratitude for your great services towards me let me display before the eyes of all men my public acknowledgement that you saved my life.

When peace had been restored throughout the world and the lawful political order re-established, we began to enjoy quiet and happy times. It is true that we did wish to have children who had for some time been denied us by an envious fate. Had it pleased Fortune to continue her usual favour to us, what would have been lacking to either of us?

The speaker and his late wife are clearly well-known and

Some inscriptions

well-connected (that much is clear from the lines just quoted) and the attention they attracted in the proscription of 43 was presumably on account of their wealth. Nothing suggests, though, that the speaker was of senatorial rank, though such rank was in itself no guarantee of competence as a speaker (Cic. *Brut.* 233, 267). The text has been minutely studied: it reveals nothing whatever of its author's reading or thinking; a flat and repetitious lexicon is the natural result. The funeral oration was, according to Cicero, no place for rhetorical display (*De orat.* 2.341), though our fragments of such orations do in practice undermine that judgement. But our speaker is so sparing of ornament as to raise doubts: there is no more than a scatter of the preferred rhythmical sentence-ends, or of alliteration and assonance, or of (for example) rhetorical questions. Sentences are awkwardly constructed, with no more than passing hints of flowing, elegant parallelisms (try from *pedes prostrata* to *corporis repleta*). The speaker evidently wrote his own text and it is likely that the stones even preserve his marks of punctuation. He writes baldly, from the heart, but it is the absence of of any remembered glow of style or language to elevate his grief that strikes all serious critics of these lines.

(2) *Inscr. Lat. Sel.* 8394. *Laudatio Murdiae*,[2] lines 15-31. Another funeral *laudatio*, again of a woman, perhaps a very few years later.

> Constitit ergo in hoc sibi ipsa ut a parentibus dignis viris data matrimonia opsequio probitate retineret, nupta meriteis gratior fieret, fide carior haberetur, iudicio orna-

Appendix 2

tior relinqueretur, post decessum consensu civium laudaretur, quom descriptio partium habeat gratum fidumque animum in viros, aequalitatem in liberos, iustitiam in veritate.

Quibus de causeis quom omnium bonarum feminarum simplex similisque esse laudatio soleat, quod naturalia bona propria custodia servata varietates verborum non desiderent, satisque sit eadem omnes bona fama digna fecisse, et quia adquirere novas laudes mulieri sit arduom. quom minoribus varietatibus vita iactetur, necessario communia esse colenda, ne quod amissum ex iustis praecepteis cetera turpet.

Eo maiorem laudem omnium carissima mihi mater meruit, quod modestia probitate pudicitia opsequio lanificio diligentia fide par similisque cetereis probeis feminis fuit, neque ulli cessit virtutis laboris sapientiae periculorum praecipuam aut certe [nulli secundam memoriam sibi parans].

So she was in this consistent with herself that she retained two marriages given (to her) by her parents to worthy men by obedience and probity that she, as a married woman, by her merits became more agreeable (*or* acceptable, *gratior*), that by her loyalty she became dearer, that by her (sc. testamentary) judgement she was left more honoured. After her decease she was praised by the agreement of the citizens. Since the allocation of shares displays a grateful and loyal spirit towards her husbands, fairness towards her children and justice in a true cause.

For which reasons, since the funeral tribute of all good

Some inscriptions

women should be simple and similar, because their natural excellences, guarded by their own custody, do not require variations in language and since it is enough that all have done the same things worthy of a good reputation, and because it is difficult for a woman to acquire original themes for praise, because their life is tossed by lesser vicissitudes, it (follows) necessarily that conventional virtues should be pursued, lest what is lost from the best principles should debase the remainder.

Hereby my mother, dearest to me, won the greatest praise of all, in that in modesty, decency, chastity, obedience, woolmaking, zeal and loyalty, she was like and similar to other good women nor yielded to any, (having attained) the chief or at least an equal glory from her labours, wisdom, dangers.

Here we are still within the equestrian order, but at a perceptibly more modest level, but the cultural attainment is more complex: the writer produces the rhythmically impeccable (by the standards of Cicero and Quintilian) *probitate retineret* alongside the deplorable, hexameter-like *cetera turpet*; the first sentence begins and ends with quite elaborate series of parallel clauses (comparative adj. + noun in abl. + imperf. subj., three times over; at the end, three nouns in acc., each + in + acc., except for the last, where I cannot explain or, really, translate, *in ueritate*). An author, therefore, with some faint idea of 'Ciceronian' arrangement and rules, but no skill or experience in the execution. One superlative, *carissima*, is admitted. *Varietates* is over-used (as are other words elsewhere in the text); limited vocabulary is required, the writer tells us,

Appendix 2

by the occasion, but those limits easily lapse into mere repetition. Paradoxically, then, this *laudator* is a slightly more advanced writer than our first text, though clearly of a nearly-comparable training.

(3) *CIL* 11.600 (C. Castricius).³ Early Augustan, from Forlì, fifty miles ESE of Bologna. Castricius may have returned to the land, or may only have taken up farming on the land allotted him at retirement.

C. Castricius T. f. Calvus trib(unus) [mil(itum) leg(ionis...] Stellatina [Agr]icola bonoru[m libertorum] benevolus [patronus] maxsimeque eorum, qui agros bene [et strenue colant, qui] corporis cultus, quod maxime opus est [agricolis, curam gerant], qui se alant, cetera quaequomque habe[nt tueantur].

Praecepta vera, qui volt ver[e] bene et libere v[ivere, haec habeto:]

Primum est pium esse; [domino bene] cupias, ver[ere parentes ... f]idem bonam [praestes, ... noli maledicere ne male] audias. Inn[ocens et fidus qui erit,] suavem vitam [et offensa carentem] hon[este l]ae[teque] peraget.

Haec non a d[octeis vireis institutus, sed n]atura sua e[t us]u Agricola meminisse docet vos.

L. Castricio L(uci) C(ai) l(iberto) ... ob merita quod eius mortem dolui et fu[nus feci et locum dedi, ide]mque monumentum hoc et feci, ut cu[rent omnes liberti fidem pr]aestare patroneis; item Ca]striciae C(ai) l(ibertae) Helenae, quod et [ipsa pia fuit.

Some inscriptions

C. Castricius Calvus, son of Titus, military tribune of the – legion, of the Stellatine tribe, Agricola ['farmer'; apparently an *agnomen*, like Sulla *Felix*], the kindly patron of good freedmen, and in particular of those who till the fields well and energetically, who take care of the body's upkeep, which is particularly necessary for farmers, who look after themselves and watch over the other things they have. Who wishes to live in truth well and freely, let him hold these true precepts.

First, to be dutiful, wish your patron well and respect your parents ... Keep good faith ... Do not speak ill lest ill be spoken of you. Whoever shall be harmless and loyal will lead decently and cheerfully a pleasant life without trouble.

Agricola, taught not by wise men but by his nature and experience bids you remember ...

[Castricius goes on to describe the erection of a monument to his freedman Lucius and freedwoman Helena.]

This fragmentary Augustan text has attracted much attention because of its alleged relevance to veteran settlement, Augustan agricultural policy and the background to Virgil's *Georgics*. There is no serious evidence that that policy ever existed (cf. Horsfall (1995), 69), no case therefore that Virgil was that policy's spokesman, and certainly no link between the poet's attitude and Castricius! The lumbering, traditional phrasing might be Castricius' own, but style and language give nothing away. Proverbs and maxims were dear to the Romans, as graffiti, funerary inscriptions and the many inscriptions on backgammon boards make plain;[4] collections have come

Appendix 2

down to us (the *Dicta Catonis*, the *Sententiae* of Publilius Syrus) and Castricius might (or might not) have consulted an anthology. The tone is one often associated with the moralising expressed by and attributed to, the elder Cato. The content is sometimes close to Cato's own *de agri cultura*, sometimes closer to the moralising found in epitaphs. Some of Castricius' farm staff may have been able to read these maxims,[5] others probably not, but I do not speculate upon their likely reaction; the text is more important as witness to conservatism of thought and language in the countryside of Augustan Italy.

(4) *Inscr. Lat. Sel.* 5795. (Nonius Datus).[6] The military engineer Nonius Datus' report on his second intervention (AD 152) on the water-supply of Saldae is preserved as part of a long inscribed dossier.

... Profectus sum et inter vias latrones sum passus; nudus saucius evasi cum meis; Saldas veni; Clementem procuratorem conveni. Ad montem me perduxit; ube cuniculum dubii operis flebant, quasi relinquendus habebatur, ideo quod perforatio operis cuniculi longior erat effect., quam montis spatium. Apparuit fossuras a rigorem errasse, adeo ut superior fossura dextram petit ad meridiem versus, inferior similiter dextram suam petit at septentrionem: duae ergo partes relicto rigore errabant. Rigor autem depalatus erat supra montem ab orientem in occidentem. Ne quis tamen legenti error fiat de fossuris, quot est scriptum 'superior' et 'inferior', sic intellegamus: 'superior' est pars, qua cuniculus aquam recipit, inferior qua emittit. Cum opus adsignar., ut

Some inscriptions

scirent, quis quem modum suum perforationis haber., certamen operis inter classicos milites et gaesates dedi et sic ad compertusionem montis conuener ....

I departed and on the way suffered bandits; stripped and wounded I got away with my team/escort (?). I reached Saldae. I met Varius Clemens. He took me to the mountain, where they were crying over a tunnel of doubtful workmanship which they thought had to be abandoned because the penetration of the excavation work had been carried further than the width of the mountain. It was apparent that the excavations had strayed, so that the upstream work turned right (to S.) and the downstream work to *its* right, to N. So the two ends had lost their line and gone astray. The line had been staked out over the mountain from E. to W. So the reader shall not be mistaken about the tunnelling, 'upper' indicates where the tunnel receives the water, 'lower' where it emits. When I was assigning the work, so that they might know who had what quota of digging, I started a competition between the soldiers of the fleet and the javelin-troops [see *OLD* s.v. *gaesates*] and so they linked up where the mountain was pierced.

The language of narrative inscriptions (cf. *Inscr. Lat. Sel.* index, VIIM) has not been sufficiently studied: Nonius Datus' matter and manner are remarkable, moments in the hectic life of a specialist army engineer, distracted by bandits from the important business of aqueducts and tunnels. Just after AD 150, in North Africa, the system seems not to have functioned

Appendix 2

well. Except, perhaps for ND's training in writing reports: note the pedantic insistence on the correct sense of 'upper' and 'lower'. Throughout, the sense is beautifully clear (though the matter is not entirely simple) and ND's prose is meticulously organised on three principles: object near the beginning, verb near the end, and ('asyndeton') avoidance of connexions between sentences. Rather like Caesar, indeed. That may mean that specialist officers were trained to write reports in the flawless manner of the best military prose, or else that ND's senior clerk was exceptionally skilled. Either way, the text shows how the army could function as a teacher of flawless technical narrative, if not of flawless grammar.

(5) *CLE* 1988 (Allia Potestas), vv. 11-25.[7] This text (perhaps *c.* AD 200) is the epitaph of a freedwoman, Allia Potestas, who cohabited successfully with two men simultaneously. Only one of them, though, commemorates her charms and virtues.

> exiguo sermone inreprehensa manebat.
> prima toro delapsa fuit, eadem ultima lecto
> se tulit ad quietem positis ex ordine rebus.
> lana cui e manibus nuncquam sine caussa recessit.
> opsequioque prior nulla moresque salubres.
> haec sibi non placuit, numquam sibi libera uisa.
> candida, luminibus pulchris, aurata capillis,
> et nitor in facie permansit eburneus illae,
> qualem mortalem nullam habuisse ferunt.
> pectore et in niueo breuis illi forma papillae.
> quid crura? Atalantes status illi comicus ipse.
> anxia non mansit, sed corpore pulchra benigno.

Some inscriptions

levia membra tulit, pilus illi quaesitus ubique.
quod manibus duris fuerit culpabere forsan.

She stayed uncensured because there was little gossip. She slipped from her bed first of them all and likewise she was the last there to return to rest, when affairs had been set in order. The wool never left her hands without reason. No one was before her in deference or sound morals. She never had a high opinion of herself and never thought herself a free woman. She was lovely, with beautiful eyes, and golden hair; there was an ivory gleam in her face such as they say no mortal had. And on her snowy breast the shape of her nipples was small (?). What of her legs? The very stance of Atalanta on the comic stage. She was not sparing but generous with her lovely body. She kept her limbs smooth and sought out her hair everywhere. That she had hard hands you will perhaps reprove her ....

Readers familiar with the hexameters of Virgil and Ovid are urged not to try reading these lines; they will fail! Their author has an uncertain grasp of the rules and his scansion (note line 23 *illi quaesitus* not classical tum-tum-tum-tum-di, but tum-di-di-tum-di) illustrates the passage from the classical hexameter to mediaeval accentual verse. *Manebat* for *erat* (11, 22), *delapsa fuit* for *delapsa est* (12), *caussa* with shortened a (14), *illae* for *illi* (18) are typical of the age, not signs of a weak education, though a trained author would have avoided, we hope, the uncertain sense of v. 20 (is *papilla* 'breast', or 'nipple'?). Actually the author knew his Ovid intimately (and

Appendix 2

just possibly Propertius, Tibullus too). And he went to the theatre: Atalanta on the comic stage points to the mythological plots of mime, in a very specific direction, for the mimic stage delighted in explicit sexuality (cf. 124, n. 35). Better yet, according to the author's beloved Ovid, Atalanta found uses other than athletic for her splendidly-trained physique (*Am.* 3.2.29, *Ars* 3.775). Our extraordinary poem praises Allia's housework, and legwork; its author no longer writes conventional hexameters, yet can employ an allusion to Ovid to suggest the uses to which Allia put those flawless limbs, even in an epitaph, not an epitaph cobbled out of a stonemason's little book of commonplaces but rather, a remarkable mirror of one man's reading and of an age of linguistic transition.

Notes

1. Song and memory

1. *Conf.* 1.13.22.
2. On memorisation at Rome, cf. Horsfall (1991), 61f., J.P. Small, *Wax tablets of the mind* (London 1997), 123 (use with care: cf. my review, *Journ. Rom. Arch.* 11 (1998), 566f.); see too Th. Klauser, *Reallex. Ant. Christ.* 1, 1030-9, Ph. Borgeaud, 'Memory' in *Encyclopaedia of Religion* (ed. M. Eliade) 9 (New York 1987), 370, H. Blum, *Die antike Mnemotechnik* (*Spudasmata* 15, Hildesheim 1969), 136ff., Mary Carruthers, *The book of memory* (Cambridge 1990), 18ff. For the use of jingles, cf. W.J.F. Davies, *Teaching reading in early England* (Bath 1973), 73ff., W.J. Ong, *Orality and literacy* (London 1982), 34.
3. Macr. 1.24.5; cf. *SHA Clod. Alb.* 5.2.
4. Oros. 1.18. On how Virgil was read in antiquity, see Horsfall (1995), 250f..
5. Cic. *Leg.* 2.59, Hier. *Ep.* 107.4.2.
6. Quint. 11.2.1ff., T. Morgan, *Literate education* (Cambridge 1998), 250f..
7. D.H. Fowler, *ZPE* 53 (1983), 263f., 75 (1988), 273ff., 105 (1995), 225ff., R. Cribiore, *Gymnastics of the mind* (Princeton 2001), 180ff., MacMullen (1976), 58.
8. See Brink on Hor. *Ars* 325ff.. Hor. writes of *longis rationibus*; Hultsch may be right in thinking that the Roman way of writing numbers out in full (as against using numerals) was inherently long, or slow. The tables will also, we may suspect, have been full of arcane, rarely-used fractions.
9. See F. Hultsch, *NJhb.* 139 (1889), 335ff.; more accessible, Brink *cit.*, Horsfall (1989), 204, *id.* (1991), 64; cf. Bonner (1977), 181ff..

10. See Friedlaender's comm. (1891), Horsfall (1989), 203f.; quite misunderstood, Bonner (1977), 183. Note the little pet at Petr. 46.4 who can already divide by 4; at 75.3 Trimalchio's own *puer* can divide by 10: first steps, but towards a lucrative future after fondling. Sums seem central in this society.
11. Cf. p. 43.
12. See Wiseman (1998), 69, Purcell (1994), 683, E. Rawson (ch. 4, n. 48), 260, Wille (1967), 127.
13. Controversial: my friend Ramsay MacMullen, *Historia* 40 (1991), 420ff. does not convince me here; see Horsfall (1993), 801, n. 4 and still L.R. Taylor, *Trans. Am. Philol. Assoc.* 68 (1937), 301.
14. F. Ritschl, *Parerga zu Plautus und Terenz* (Leipzig 1845), 306ff., Duckworth (1952), 77f. (cf. 65ff. for revivals); several plays in a day: cf. W. Beare, *Roman stage*[2] (London 1955), 166. 'Endless repetitions of flawed originals' could as well describe a flood of recent books on the Roman theatre; I cite sparingly.
15. Jory (1987), 145. The Theatre of Pompey 55 BC, Theatre of Marcellus, 17 BC, Theatre of Balbus, 13 BC; overcrowded, Hor. *Ep.* 1.19.41f., 2.1.60, *Ars* 205.
16. Jory (1987), 144, Wiseman (1985), 45f., for the *ludi compitalicii*.
17. The *docta ... carmina* which *iuvenes* and *puellae* learned *per urbem* at Stat. *Silv.* 1.2.172-3 seem to be prep., not fun. At Hor. *Ep.* 2.1.59f. we read of *Roma potens* that learns by heart Plautus, Terence, Caecilius: *in scholis* comments our best ancient annotator, Porphyrio, and that is confirmed by Cicero (*Tusc. Disp.* 2.27, 3.3) and Quintilian (1.1.36): see Brink's note on Hor. *Ep* 2.1.59f..
18. Conventions: E.W. Handley, *Dioniso* 46 (1975), 117ff. (in English), Chalmers (1965), 21ff.. Allusions: not one applicable to modern times that the audience missed or that the actors failed to play up, Cic. *Sest.* 118; cf. Wright (1931), 4ff., Yavetz (1988), 18ff., E. Tengström, *Eranos* 75 (1977), 43ff., Wiseman (1985), 37, Nicolet (1976), 479ff., Cameron (1976), 158ff., Aldrete (1999), 144.
19. Hor. *Ep.* 2.1.186 calls it *plebecula*, little *plebs* (and cf. Chapter 2, p. 26 for such designations); actually the audience was a total social mix, see p. 58.
20. Suet. *Galba* 13; see Ribbeck, *Com. Rom. Frag.* p. 274, but we have no real idea of what the words repeated really were.
21. Cf. Pacuvius *Trag.* frag. 197 (in Ribbeck's ed., *Trag. Rom. Frag.*),

Hor. *Sat.* 2.3.60 (with Muecke's notes): a delicate and controversial problem; Cicero returned to Pacuvius' scene repeatedly.

22. Klingshirn (1994), 184-6, Horsfall (1991), 74, Klauser and Borgeaud (*cit.* n. 2), G. Rietschel, *Lehrbuch der Liturgik* 2 (Berlin 1909), 29ff..

23. Caesarius was Bishop of Arles, 502-42, and his sermons are richly informative on the issue of memory: I summarise here Klingshirn (1994), 184f., handier than the indices of Dom Morin's ed. in two vast volumes (*Corp. Christ.* 103, 104 (1953), reprinting ed. 1, Maredsous 1937, 1942.

24. Cf. E. Starobinski-Safran in *La mémoire des religions* ed. P. Borgeaud (Geneva 1988), 79ff., B. Gerhardsson, *Memory and manuscript* (Uppsala 1961), 113ff., F. Schürer, *History of the Jewish people* 2 (2nd ed., with G. Vermes, F. Millar, etc., Edinburgh 1979), 415ff..

25. The officiant 'gives the lead', *praeit*, in words and gestures; the words are variously *sollemnia, certa, concepta*, 'ritual, fixed, formal' (G. Wissowa, *Religion und Kultus der Römer* (2nd ed., München 1912), 394f., 397).

26. *Serm. Guelf.* 1.11 (*Patr. Lat.* Suppl. 2.543); cf. Rietschel (*cit.* n. 22).

27. Caesarius, *Serm.* 238.1, etc., Klingshirn (1994) 184f..

28. Cf. Klingshirn (1994), 198, 216, and for later periods, 284, 285. See Caesarius *Serm.* 13.4, 16.3, 130.4, 130.5, etc.; the material is abundant.

29. Hier. *Epist.* 21.13 *comoedias legere, amatoria bucolicorum versuum verba cantare, tenere Vergilium*, Horsfall (1995), 250f., Wille (1967), 226.

30. Aug. *Serm.* 241.5 (*Patr. Lat.* 38.1135f.) *pauci nostis in libris, multi in theatris*.

31. H. Reich, *Der Mimus* (Berlin 1903), 746ff., J. Quasten *Musik und Gesang* ... (Münster 1930), 186ff., G. Wille in *Augustinus-Lexicon* (ed. C. Mayer, etc.) 1 (Basel 1986-94), 725, Jürgens (1972), 194, n. 3.

32. Horsfall (1995), 250f..

33. *Inst.* 6.20.27 *comicae fabulae de stupris uirginum*.

34. *Ad uxorem* 2.6.11f..

35. Cf. Jürgens (1972), Weismann (1972), H.A. Kelly, *Traditio* 35 (1979), 21ff., T.D. Barnes in *Roman theater and society* ed. W. Slater (Ann Arbor 1996), 161ff. and the commentaries of E. Castorina and M. Turcan on Tert. *Spect.*: it is almost impossible to work out from the Fathers' denunciations just what they could actually have gone to see in the theatre; mime or pantomime only, we suspect, at least from

the end of the 'archaising' period. Cf. Bonaria (1965) for the fragments of (panto)mime down to the late empire.
36. Hier. *In Eph.* 3.6.4 (*Patr. Lat.* 26.540A); cf. Jürgens (1972), 86, n. 6.
37. Augustine *de opere monachorum* 17.20 (*Patr. Lat.* 40.565).
38. Cf. Wille (1967), 123 with nn. 213, 218, Arbesmann (1972), 35 with n. 136, *Thes. Ling. Lat.* 3.759.3-10; see e.g. Isidore, *Eccl. Off.* 2.16.2 (*Patr. Lat.* 83.800A) *canunt autem manibus operantes et ipsum laborem, tamquam divino celeumate, consolantur.*
39. Hier. *Epist.* 46.12 (*CSEL* 54.342f.), A. Hamman, *La vie quotidienne en Afrique du Nord au temps de Saint Augustin* (Paris 1985), 227.
40. Wille *cit.*; cf. John Chrysostom *In psal.* 41 (*Patr. Graec.* 55. 156); for N. Africa, see Arbesmann (1972), for Gaul, Sid. Ap. *Epist.* 2.10.25-30, 8.12.5.
41. See Basil, *Regulae fusius tractatae* 37.2 (*Patr. Graec.* 31.1012), Aug. *Epist.* 211.7 (*Patr. Lat.* 33.960), *Regula magistri* 50 (*Patr. Lat.* 50.25), *Regula Tarnatensis* 10 (*Patr. Lat.* 66.981D).
42. See n. 37; Aug. continues: *an ignoramus omnes opifices quibus vanitatibus et plerumque etiam turpitudinibus theatricarum fabularum donent corda et linguas suas cum manus ab opere non recedant?* Cf. Wille (1967), 153, Arbesmann (1972), 35 with n. 136, Hammann (*cit.* n. 39), C. Hoeg, *Byzantion* 25/7 (1955/7), 392.
43. Horsfall (1989), 197f.; Wille (1967), 108f. quite undervalues the importance of music in Petronius. For Greece, far more richly documented, cf. M.L. West, *Ancient Greek music* (Oxford 1992), 27ff. K. Bücher, *Arbeit und Rhythmus* (many edd.); the fragments collected, D. Page, *Poetae melici graeci*, 450ff..
44. Harris (1989), 285ff., MacMullen (1976), 58f..
45. Horsfall (1991), 73, Klingshirn (1994), 183f..
46. *Serm.* 6.3; cf. nn. 22, 23, 28.
47. *Serm.* 19.3; cf. 16.3, Klingshirn (1994), 198. Lewd songs: *Serm.* 13.4, 16.3, 19.3, 33.4, 130.5.

2. Rules of evidence

1. H. Lausberg, *Handbuch der literarischen Rhetorik* 1 (München 1960), 425.
2. The first time I tried to explain why these difficulties were rewarding, rather than crushing, a reviewer (C. Moatti, *RPh.* 71 (1997), 204f.) spotted, perhaps even in the English summary in

Horsfall (1996), 58ff., the possible objections I had anticipated, and restated them quite amply, while suppressing any word of my response to them, and offering no further comment on the book! This was an easy and original way of filling a page in a learned journal. Cf. Matt. 25.21.

3. 280ff. in the reprint of 1964, Stuttgart.
4. D. West, *The imagery and poetry of Lucretius* (Edinburgh 1969), 64ff..
5. M. Coffey, *Bull. Inst. Class. Stud.* 8 (1961), 63ff..
6. Sen. *Epist. Mor.* 56; see P. Fedeli, *La natura violata* (Palermo 1980), 95.
7. Cf. G. Highet, *Anatomy of satire* (Princeton 1962), 24ff..
8. Cf. *Class. Rev.* 43 (1993), 269, *Inv. Luc.* 13-14 (1991-2), 172f., *Riv. Fil.* 125 (1997), 170ff., on Calpurnius Siculus. Betty Radice (Penguin ed., Pliny, *Letters*, 25) remarks on Pliny's 'observant eye and retentive memory'.
9. Cf. pp. 43 and 106.
10. Cf. Coffey (*cit.* n. 5).
11. G. Zanker, *Realism in Alexandrian poetry* (Beckenham 1987), A. Perutelli in Horsfall (1995), 46f., N. Tarleton, *Class. Quart.* 39 (1989), 267ff..
12. *Class. Med.* 52 (2001), 303ff..
13. Z. Yavetz in Seager (1969), 162ff., Brunt (1966), 11ff., A. Scobie, *Klio* 68 (1986), 399ff..
14. See pp. 43 and 45. For full details of the older handbooks of Roman daily life, cf. S. Treggiari, *Roman social history* (London 2002), H. Blanck, *Einführung in das Privatleben der Griechen und Römer*[2] (Darmstadt 1996).
15. Underwear: Cic. *Off.* 1.129 and Plin. *Nat.* 12.59 do not permit generalisation; L. Wilson, *Clothing of the ancient Romans* (Baltimore 1938), 71ff., L. Bonfante Warren, *Aufstieg und Niedergang* ... 1.4 (Berlin 1973), 597f.. Headgear: not the hood (*cucullus*) of the cloak (*paenula*), or at least not in Rome: cf. Cic. *Sest.* 82, Colum. 1.8.9, Mart. 14.139.
16. Ch. 3, nn. 40, 41. Cf. Courtney (1993), 470ff. ('*uersus populares*'), Cupaiuolo (1993),134ff..
17. Wiedemann (1992), 55ff., D.G. Kyle, *Spectacles of death* (London 1998), 50f., J.C. Golvin, *L'amphithéâtre romain* 1 (Paris 1988), 265ff., G. Ville, *La gladiature en occident* (Roma 1981), 125f.. Diversity of arms and armour made variation easier: Friedlaender, *SG* 4, 258ff..

18. J.H. Humphrey, *Roman circuses* (London 1986), 592ff., Cameron (1976), 3 *et passim* ('some change').
19. See Chapter 1, n. 35, Wiedemann (1992), 128ff..
20. See D. Birley, *Social history of English cricket* (London 1999), R.Guha, *Corner of a foreign field: the Indian history of a British sport* (London 2002).
21. J. Fontaine s.v. *Hymn, Hymnology* in *Encyclopedia of the early church* ed. A. di Berardino (Cambridge 1992), 401, Lane Fox (1986), 360f., MacMullen (1981), 15ff., *id.* (1984), 74f.. Against the hypothesis of a musical continuity between Jews/Pagans and Christians, see C. Hannick, *New Grove dictionary of music and musicians* 4 (London 1980), 365, 370.
22. O. Hirschfeld, *Kleine Schriften* (Berlin 1913), 682ff., P. Maas, *Byz. Ztschr.* 21 (1912), 28ff., A. Alföldi, *Mitt. Deut. Arch. Inst.* 49 (1934), 79ff., Th. Klauser, *Reallex. Ant. Christ.* 1 (Stuttgart 1950), s.v. 'Akklamation', cols 221ff., C.M. Roueché, *Journ. Rom. Stud.* 74 (1984), 181ff., S.G. MacCormack, *Art and ceremony in late antiquity* (Berkeley 1981), 23, with n. 31, Aldrete (1999), 104ff..
23. M.J. Jeffreys, *Dumbarton Oaks Papers* 28 (1974), 184, 189. It is comforting to find a very similar line of argument in Purcell (1994), 663, with n. 74.
24. Cf. MacMullen (1997), 47f., *id.* (1981), 16ff..
25. Note the familiar history of the Libre vermeill de Monserrat.
26. *Oral tradition and written record* (Cambridge 1989), *Literacy and orality* (Cambridge 1992). Her remark in the latter, p. 158, that the world of Roman history 'has remained unruffled by the controversies surrounding orality' was no longer even quite fair when written (see next n.).
27. Cf. many of the contributions to two volumes ed. by G. Vogt-Spira, *Strukturen der Mündlichkeit in der römischen Literatur* (Tübingen 1990), *Beiträge zur mündlichen Kultur der Römer* (Tübingen 1993). On the former, cf. my remarks, *Riv. Fil.* 121 (1993), 81ff..
28. Cf. Chapter 3, n. 13.
29. Cf. D. Liebs in Vogt-Spira (*cit.* n. 27), 83ff., Harris (1989), 198f.. Long known, though: cf. e.g. F. Schulz, *History of Roman legal science* (Oxford 1946), 25f..
30. On the refined musical ear of a Roman crowd, cf., eloquently, Dupont (1985), 115f. (cf. Habinek (1998), 36f., without evidence). We are all dependent upon Wille (1967); cf. further Chapter 3, n. 2.
31. Cf. W.J. Ong, *Orality and literacy* (London 1982), 62f., V.E.

Neuburg, *Popular literature* (Harmondsworth 1977), 236f., Richard Hoggart, *Uses of literacy* (Harmondsworth 1986), 149ff., J. Vansina, *Oral tradition* (Harmondsworth 1973), 39.
32. (1988), 141ff. ('semantic difficulties').
33. See too Purcell (1994), 646ff., Mouritsen (2001), 39ff., Millar (1998), 13ff., *id.* (2002), 136ff., 208ff., Brunt (1966), 3ff., *id.* (1971), 127ff., MacMullen (1974) 57ff..
34. Cf. Yavetz (1988), 149, and *id.*, *Athen.* 43 (1965), 295ff., Hellegouarc'h (1963), 506ff.. For the opprobium, cf. Mouritsen (2001), 139ff., and see Chapter 7.
35. Cf. Cic. *Sest.* 118 *universus populus*, *Tusc. Disp.* 1.106 *totis theatris*, *Att.* 2.19.3. Plut. *Cic.* 13.4 relates an occasion when the theatre public was divided. Likewise 'the whole Roman people': see Mouritsen (2001), 13, n. 44, Cic. *Pis.* 7, etc. 'All over the town', of an allusive graffito at Terracina.
36. Purcell (1994), 675.
37. S. Stone in *World of Roman costume* ed. J.L. Sebesta, L. Bonfante (Madison 2001), 13.
38. Cf. MacMullen (1974), 193, n. 55 on further refinements of insignia at the top end of the scale. On Ovid, cf. Wiseman (1998), 69(!).
39. Cic. *De orat.* 3.42ff., Ramage (1973), 67ff.; cf. Appendix 2, p. 119.
40. Cf. p. 116ff. for some new evidence to this effect.
41. At the level of the freedmen in Petronius, *lucrum* was altogether desirable (cf. 58.11, 61.3, J.H. D'Arms, *Commerce and social standing ...* (Cambridge, Mass. 1981), 119, n. 92, T. McGinn, *Mem. Amer. Acad. Rome* 42 (1997), 107f., R.P. Saller, B.D. Shaw, *Journ. Rom. Stud.* 74 (1984), 127f., J.-P. Morel, in *L'uomo romano* ed. A. Giardina (Bari 1993), 296); higher up the ladder, snobbery and circumlocution triumphed: cf. D'Arms, 60 and my note (Oxford 1989) on Nepos *Atticus* 14.3, for two recent attempts to separate disdainful theory from greedy and more tolerant reality. See too e.g. Vanderbroeck (1987), 19.
42. Cf. Hor. *Epist.* 1.1.58, Millar (1998), 203f..
43. Cf. Purcell (1994), 657, 663, 675, Vanderbroeck (1987), 52ff.; an old idea: cf. Tac. *Hist.* 1.4.
44. Purcell's world (1994, 659ff.) of the shopkeepers (*tabernarii*) and working men's associations (*collegia*) I think I understand; we may be indeed writing about the same plebeians. Cf. Millar (1998), 14ff., 30ff., Mouritsen (2001), 38ff., 143ff. For loyalties to trade and

neighbourhood, cf. Purcell (1994), 674, MacMullen (1974), 135ff., Vanderbroeck (1987), 87, Lintott (1968), 77ff., Nippel (1995), 71ff..
45. Cf. Purcell (1994), 673.
46. Reading of the last fifty lines of the epistle is warmly recommended. I wrote a short book about it (and my friend Volteius), *La villa sabina di Orazio* (Venosa 1993), but it is unfortunately not generally available. Volteius belongs strictly *c.* 90 BC; truly, he is timeless.
47. Juvenal's inheritors make another chilling study: see Tosi (1991), 477n° 1026 for (e.g.) Lorenzo the Magnificent's (attributed) 'pane e feste tengono il popol quieto'.
48. G. Lumbroso, *L'Egitto al tempo dei Greci e dei Romani*² (Roma 1895), 111f.; see too the commentaries of Courtney, Mayor and Friedlaender on Juv. 10.81, *id.*, *SG* 2, 2.
49. Jos. *c. Ap.* 2.5.60; cf. App. *Civ.* 4.262, 269.
50. Cf. P.M. Fraser, *Ptolemaic Alexandria* 2 (Oxford 1972), 95f., n. 213, 100, n. 231; the Alexandrians' passion for horseracing: Polyb. 5.37.7 and Lumbroso (*cit.* n. 48).
51. *Orat.* 32.31.
52. *Knights* 1207f., *Plutus* 1164ff., V. Ehrenberg, *People of Aristophanes* (Oxford 1951), 242f., 252.
53. So a Jewish observer was struck, Jos. *Ant. Iud.* 19.1.16.130; see too Juv. 8.117 (again with the commentaries, n. 48), Tac. *Ann.* 1.2, *Hist.* 1.4 (with Yavetz, n. 34), 4.38, Fronto p. 213.12vdH². Note too *gaudia*, pleasure for the *populus* commemorated on a travelling actor's epitaph, *ILLRP* 804.2, with Rawson (1991), 485, and Volteius Mena, *gaudentem*, taking pleasure in the *ludi*, which at this date meant circus or theatre, Hor. *Ep.* 1.7.59.
54. Cf., for example, Hdt. 3.81, [Xen.] *Ath. Pol.* 1.4ff., Cic. *Rep.* 2.39: see Walbank on Polyb. 6.3.8, ch. 4 of N. Loraux, *Invention of Athens* (Eng. tr., Cambridge, Mass., 1986), Millar (1998), 203. 'Give them council housing? They only put coal in the bath' is a hoary old slander in just the same tradition; its black history perhaps deserves study.
55. MacMullen (1974), 138ff., Hellegouarc'h (1963), 525ff., Mouritsen (2001), 139ff..
56. Dregs: Cic. *Pis.* 9, *QFr.* 2.5.3; 'scoundrel' I use in place of the regular *malus/impius/improbus*.
57. A useful introduction, Nisbet's comm. on Cic. *Pis.* (Oxford 1961), 192ff..
58. Cf. Mouritsen (2001), 139-41.
59. 1.8.2 *socors et somniculosum genus id mancupiorum, otiis,*

campo, circo, theatris, aleae, popinae, lupanaribus consuetum. Energetically expanded, Amm. Marc. 14.6.25f.; cf. Purcell (1995), 17f..
60. Cf. Cic. *Phil.* 13.24 *lustris popinis alea vino*; Mark Antony given to brothels, cookshops, dicing, wine; cf. *Cat.* 2.23, *Sest.* 20, *Phil.* 3.35, Opelt (1965), 158f..
61. My introduction to the issues, *Lat.* 30 (1971), 1108ff. reprinted, *Oxford readings in Vergil's Aeneid* (ed. S.J. Harrison, Oxford 1990), 305ff.. Some expansion, M. Dickie, *Pap. Liv. Lat. Sem.* 5 (1985), 165ff.. See too W. Heitland, *Agricola* (Cambridge 1921) and Powell's notes on Cic. *Sen.* 24, 55.
62. In glorious detail, Purcell (1995), 3ff..
63. Alternatives to school: Horsfall (1991), 63f.. Alternatives to literacy: cf. Horsfall (1998), 565ff..

3. Music returns to Rome

1. Cf. Chapter 2, n. 30.
2. Friedlaender, *SG* 2, 161-88 was valuable pioneering work; throughout I cite *SG* ed. 9-10 (Leipzig 1919-1921); the English tr. is only of the 7th ed., and is markedly inferior to the later, amplified edition of the original. Wille (1967) is a vast and fundamental survey (in German); add now Maria Paola Guidobaldi, *Musica e danza, Vita e costumi dei Romani antichi* 13 (Roma 1992), with a fine selection of illustrations.
3. Which used to be attributed to Virgil but belongs pretty clearly to the late first century AD. Text in the *Appendix Vergiliana*, for which see e.g. Virgil, Loeb ed. vol. 2; here see the comm. by F.R.D. Goodyear, *Bull. Inst. Class. Stud.* 24 (1977), 119ff.; on dating, see R.J. Tarrant, *Harv. Stud. Class. Phil.* 94 (1992), 331-47.
4. For music in taverns, see also Philostratus *Hist. Apoll.* 4.42 (song), Sidonius Apollinaris 8.11.3 vv. 49-51 (song and comic love-plaints in the sausage-houses of late-antique Bordeaux; a neglected and delightful vignette), Hor. *Epist.* 1.14.25 (flute-player/ prostitute), Kleberg (1957), 117f., *id., In den Wirtshäusern und Weinstuben des antiken Rom* (Berlin 1963), 53f., Friedlander, *SG* 1, 348, Wille (1967), 144, M. Guarducci, *Acta 5th international congress ... epigraphy, Cambridge 1967* (Oxford 1971), 219ff..
5. *Cat.* 25.2; see G.M. Paul, *Pap. Liv. Lat. Seminar* 5 (1985), 9-22, B.W. Boyd, *Amer. Journ. Phil.* 117 (1987), 183-201; Macrobius *Sat.* 3.14.5 writes *Semproniam reprehendit non quod saltare sed quod*

Notes to pages 31-33

optime scierit, 'Sallust reproves Sempronia not because she dances but because she dances excellently.'
 6. See p. 34ff. below for dance; Quintilian 1.10.31 (instrumental music), Columella praef. 3-5 (music and dance), Wille, 326f., M.L. Clarke *Higher education in the ancient world* (London 1971), 52-4.
 7. Cf. Horace (*cit.* n. 4), Paul (*cit.* n. 5), 15f., H. Herter, 'Die Soziologie der antiken Prostitution', *Jahrb. Ant. Christ.* 3 (1960), 70-111 at 97f., Griffin (1985), 26f..
 8. Griffin (1985), 26f., Wille (1967), *passim*: what is written of entertainment naturally applies less to the more national and conservative music of army and religious cult. For performers, S. Treggiari, *Roman freedmen during the late republic* (Oxford 1969), 141, ead., *Amer. Journ. Anc. Hist.* 1.2 (1976), 90f., *Pap. Brit. Sch. Rome* 43 (1975), 56.
 9. Cic. *Leg.* 2.39, Varr. *Sat. Men.* 365, Hor. *Ars Poet.* 208-17 with Brink's commentary (Cambridge 1971), Sen. *Contr.* praef. 8, Sen. *De brevitate* 12.4, *Epist.* 90.19, Plin. *Nat.* 16.171, Justin 30.1.8, Amm. Marc. 14.6.18, Wille (1967), 327, Friedlaender, *SG* 2, 171ff.. For Macrobius' sketch of the moral decline in republican dance, *Saturnalia* 3.14: see p. 35.
 10. Contrast R. Hoggart, *The uses of literacy* (Harmondsworth 1981, etc.), 116ff. on Christian ethics and the English working class. C. Edwards' entertaining *The politics of immorality in ancient Rome* (Cambridge 1993) unfortunately avoids music.
 11. At least the facts have now been stated, quite fully, Horsfall (1989), 197; Wille, (1967), 108f. underestimates the evidence.
 12. Wille (1967), 143-7, J. Marquardt, A. Mau, *Das Privatleben der Römer*² (Leipzig 1886), 337, Friedlaender, *SG* 2, 173f.. Cic. *Rosc. Am.* 134 ('whole neighbourhood rings to the sound ...') confirms my suspicion that Petronius keeps a close eye upon the social realities.
 13. Cf. my discussion, 'The prehistory of Latin poetry', *Riv. Fil.* 122 (1994), 50-75 at 70ff. (a very complex problem); the account in Habinek (1998), 36ff. prefers not to engage with my analysis while Wiseman (1998), 14 offers no disagreement in detail. For equally decorous dinner music, cf. Hor. *Epodes* 9.1-6, Plin. *Epist.* 9.36.4, *SHA Hadrian* 26.4, Wille (1967), 145.
 14. Wille (1967), 143-7, Hor. *Carm.* 4.13.4ff., *cantus* and *symphoniae* in Cicero's list of counts on which to discredit Clodia, *Cael.* 35; cf. *Pro Gallio* frag. 1. See too *Cat.* 2.23.
 15. *Ib.* 25ff.; cf. J.P. Waltzing, *Étude historique sur les corporations professionnelles chez les Romains* 4 (Louvain 1900), 693, 695, E. De

Ruggiero, *Dizionario epigrafico* 2 (Roma 1900) s.v. *cena*, cols 154-6, MacMullen (1974), 132ff.. Varro *RR* 3.2.16 protests that these *cenae* are so frequent as to have pushed up the price of food.

16. Varro *RR* 2.4.20; nor was this an unusual case: cf. 3.13.1 (roe-deer), Polyb. 12.4.2ff. (Wille (1967), 111; cf. p. 103 for Seneca's army horse).

17. Cf. in general Wille (1967), 105-47. Priests: Wille (1967), 26-38; their role lavishly illustrated in I.S. Ryberg, *Rites of the state religion in Roman art* (Roma 1955): see index s.v. musicians. Shepherds: cf. Polyb. and Varro (*bis*) as cited (n. 16), Prop. 4.10.29 *pastoris bucina*, Ennodius, *carm*. 1.8, *praef.* (though many of our texts on the topic are simply expansions of the commonplaces of bucolic poetry, I cite what seems to be real evidence; see Wille (1967), 114). Soldiers: Wille (1967), 75-104, though we do not actually know if the Roman army marched in step to music: cf. the note on Verg. *Aen*. 7.698 in my commentary (Leiden 2000). Waiters: Petr. 34.1, etc. and see above, p. 111f..

18. Wille (1967), 350f.; cf. Nepos, *praef*. 1.1, *Epam*. 2.1, with my commentary, Oxford 1989, p. 113.

19. Wille (1967), 148. Quintessential background music indeed, *symphoniarum cantum ex longinquo lene resonantium*, the sound of instruments playing gently at a distance, Sen. *Dial*. 1.3.10.

20. MacMullen (1974), 139, Opelt (1965), 222.

21. Macr. *Sat*. 2.4.28; Wille (1967), 145 unfortunately and quite unacceptably attributes the story to Julius Caesar, not Augustus. Cf. my discussion of the anecdote, *Ancient History* 27 (1997), 26.

22. Cf. p. 31, A.Richlin, *Garden of Priapus*[2] (New York 1992), 54, Herter (*cit*. n. 7), 103.

23. *Orat*. frag. 30 ed. E. Malcovati, *Orat. Rom. Frag*, p. 133, A.E. Astin, *Scipio Aemilianus* (Oxford 1967), 266, frag. 53, E. Eyben, *Restless youth* (Eng. tr., London 1993), 87f..

24. Dupont (1985), 124, Opelt (1965), 158f., Wille (1967), 191-5. See e.g. *Pis*. 18 (with Nisbet's n.).

25. *Epist*. 7.24.7, etc., Wille (1967), 198f., MacMullen (1990), 146.

26. Klingshirn (1994), 198, Caes. Arel. *serm*. 16.3, 55.2, 225.5 *in sanctis festivitatibus saltare, choros ducere* to dance and perform the steps at holy festivals.

27. Good ancient pagan usage, which had survived the change of religion without missing a step, MacMullen (1981), 20ff., Wille (1967), 380-3.

28. L. Gougaud, *Dict. arch. chrét. lit.* 4 (Paris 1921), 252f., Klingshirn (1994), 217, MacMullen (1997), 103ff., 159, J. Quasten, *Musik und Gesang* (Münster 1930), 245f..

29. To argue that Italian peasants, under Augustus, really danced, on the basis of Verg. G. 1.350, Hor. *Carm.* 3.8.15f. (cf. Wille (1967), 110), is to land yourself in a dense and impenetrable thicket of literary problems (Greek sources, generic expectations and the like); it might almost be easier to argue back from e.g. Caesarius. It is, though, naturally, more likely than not on general grounds of probability that they in fact did.

30. Cf. p. 25; Wille (1967), 105, Horsfall (1987), 10, n. 70, C.O. Brink, *Horace on poetry: Epistles Book 2* (Cambridge 1982), p. 182, Cupaiuolo (1993), 135, n. 2, G. Radke, *Archaisches Latein* (Darmstadt 1981), 100ff.. Cf. (e.g.) Quint. 1.10.16, Verg. G. 1.350, Tib. 2.1.52.

31. 31.4-7, 35.6, 64.2, 73.3; cf. p. 32.

32. For whom see M.L. West, *Ancient Greek music* (Oxford 1992), 27ff.; the detailed bibliography I collected at *Riv. Fil.* 122 (1994), 63 n. 6: see above all K. Bücher, *Arbeit und Rhythmus* (many edd.).

33. *Aut si carmen conscribat, vel proponat vel cantet aliquod quod pudorem alicuius laedat*, 47.10.15.27 (the edict is far older, of course), Wille (1967), 130. For the legal issues, cf. E. Fraenkel, *Kleine Beiträge* 2 (Roma 1964), 405ff..

34. Tosi (1991), 123, n°266.

35. Cf. R.P. Saller, 'Historical anecdotes as evidence for the principate', *Greece and Rome* 27 (1980), 69-83, Wille, 130, Cupaiuolo (1993), 27. Neither saturnian nor tetrameter, though, but palpably an iambic senarius, which is not quite the metre one would expect in the context; that is no reason, however, to try to identify the line as a bizarre by-form of another metre.

36. Sen. *Epist.* 56 and Mart. 12.57 are more than enough.

37. Wille (1967), 129-31, Cupaiuolo (1993), 10-16.

38. Jocelyn Penny Small, *Wax tablets of the mind* (New York 1997), 75f..

39. Suet. *Iul.* 49.4, 80.2; for further instances of the same sort of popular political song, cf. *ib.* 80.3, *versus popularis* 1 in Courtney (1993), p. 470, *c.* 100 BC; cf. Cupaiuolo (1993), 26, n. 1.

40. Suet. *Calig.* 6.1, Courtney (1993), 478, Aldrete (1999), 138; cf. Suet. *Aug.* 98.2.

41. Cf. Cupaiuolo (1993), 134ff..

42. Cf. Suet. *Iul.* 80.3, Gell. 15.4.3 (for verses written up under statues); note too Cic. *Att.* 2.21.4, Cupaiuolo (1993), 141ff., Horsfall (1991), 70.

43. Wright (1931), 8, Cameron (1976), 158, *id.*, *Bread and circuses* (London 1973), 4, Vanderbroeck (1987), 77ff., Aldrete (1999), 104, 136f., Millar (1998), 147.

44. *Ann.* 1.16.3; Goodyear's translation (cf. Aldrete (1999), 136). *Dux* is also so used at Suet. *Nero* 20. Audience reaction had long been studied and sought – cf. Cic. *De orat.* 2.339, 3.101, *Rab. Perd.* 18 – and the forms of that reaction changed with time (on Cic. *Att.* 4.1.6, cf. Millar (2002), 177, n. 57 on the chanted repetition of a name); Suet. *Iul.* 79 *immodicas ac novas populi acclamationes* – but it was under the early empire that its rhythmic development and systematic exploitation is first attested: cf. C.M. Roueché, *Journ. Rom. Stud.* 74 (1984), 182-4, Cameron (1976), 158ff., Aldrete (1999), 101ff., 130, Vanderbroeck (1987), 114ff..

45. Cameron (n. 43, 1973), 6, cf. Yavetz (1988), 154.

46. Paul. exc. Fest. p. 76.24 Lindsay, Friedlaender, *SG* 2, 75f., Cameron (1976), 194ff., E. Pottier, DS 3.1 (Paris 1900), 230.

47. *Impari clamore*, Tac. *Ann.* 16.5, Friedlaender, *SG* 2, 142, A. Alföldi, *Mitt. Deut. Arch. Inst.* (Rome) 49 (1934), 82.

48. Tac. *Ann.* 16.5, O.F. Robinson, *Ancient Rome: city planning and administration* (London 1992), 198, Aldrete (1999), 137.

49. Tac. *ibid.*; cf. the *concentus*, 'harmony' of Plin. *Paneg.* 2.6 and the *eurythmos*, 'rhythmically', of Dio 73.2.3.

50. *Robustissimae iuventutis*, Suet. *Nero* 20.3; a.k.a *Augustiani*; cf. Aldrete (1999), 135, 141.

51. Suet. *loc. cit.*, Eyben (*cit.* n. 23), 92. Shackleton Bailey's suggestion that the shepherds' whistles of Cic. *Att.* 1.16.11 refer to hissing is not quite convincing; the passage *may* suggest rather the use of such whistles as signals for applause.

52. A. Futrell, *Blood in the arena* (Austin 1997), 165, Rawson (1991), 529, C. Roueché, *Performers and partisans at Aphrodisias*, *Journ. Rom. Stud. Monographs* 6 (1993), 124ff., at 127, MacMullen, (1975), 175, 339, n. 10.

53. Such as the *modulata carmina* ('songs set to music'; the sense is not perfectly clear) of Suet. *Aug.* 57.2; cf. Alföldi (*cit.* n. 47), 279.

54. Cameron (1976), 160, Nippel (1995), 93f., Robinson (*cit.* n. 48), 196ff., MacMullen (1975), 170ff., 339f..

55. Wright (1931), 4ff., Cameron (n. 43, 1973), 4f., (1976),

158ff., M. Wistrand, *Entertainment and violence in ancient Rome* (Göteborg 1992), 30ff.; cf. p. 85f..
56. The emphasis at MacMullen (1975), 170 is slightly different; cf . F. Millar, *Emperor in the Roman world* (London 1977), 372.
57. Cupaiuolo (1993), *passim*, Tac. *Ann.* 1.72.4, 14.48f., Suet. *Tib.* 59.1, *Nero* 38.1, etc., Courtney (1993), 475ff..
58. So Suet. *Iul.* 49.4, *Aug.* 70.2, *Calig.* 8.1, *Claud.* 1.1; cf. *Nero* 42.2 *innotuerunt*, Gell. 15.4.3. Note Val. Max. 7.5.2 for the spread of a joke, Mouritsen (2001), 116.
59. Tac. *Ann.* 1.72.4, Suet. *Aug.* 55.1, *Tib.* 28.1, Cupaiuolo (1993), 112f.
60. Cf. Tertull. *Apol.* 39, *De carne* 17, *Adv. Marc.* 5.8, H. Leclerq in *Dict. arch. chrét. lit.* 6.2 (Paris 1924), 2859-68, O. Bardenhewer *Geschichte der altchristlichen Literatur* 1² (Freiburg-i.-B. 1913), 343-83, M. Simonetti, *Studi sull' innologia popolare Mem. ... Lincei* 8.4.6 (1952), 341-484 at 375, MacMullen (1990), 391, n. 49.
61. But the distinction is fragile and unrealistic; cf. Robin Lane Fox, *Pagans and Christians* (Harmondsworth 1986), 360f..
62. *Corp. Christ.* 57.61 *volens etiam causam Donatistarum ad ipsius humillimi vulgi et omnino imperitorum atque idiotarum notitiam pervenire et eorum quantum fieri per nos posset inhaerere memoriae*, P.R.L. Brown, *Augustine of Hippo* (London 1967), 141, Simonetti (*cit.* n. 60), 375; for Irenaeus, cf. *Adv. Haer.* 1.15.6, Leclerq (*cit.* n. 60), 2850, n. 38.

4. Culture without education; education without school

1. 2.24.13; see Walbank's note, A.J. Toynbee, *Hannibal's Legacy* 1 (Oxford 1965), 260f. and Horsfall (1993), 798.
2. Cf. MacMullen (1963), 119ff., *id., Phoen.* 24 (1970), 333ff..
3. Frank (1930), 72. Cf. H. Mencken, *The American language* (4th ed., New York 1974), 573, E. Partridge, *Words, words, words* (London 1933), 135ff..
4. *Old soldier sahib* (London 1936; many reprints). For Kipling, cf. in particular *Plain tales from the hills* and *Soldiers three*. Note the vast dictionary of Anglo-Indian, H. Yule, A.C. Burrell, *Hobson-Jobson* (London 1886; many reprints). G. MacDonald Fraser's memoir of the British army in Burma, in 1944-5, *Quartered safe out here* (London 1992) still carries (227ff.) a glossary of army Hindi. B. Migliorini, *Storia della lingua italiana* (Milano 1994), 665 registers

a tiny scattering of Italian words from their brief imperial presence in Ethiopia. One might expect greater linguistic absorption to have accompanied their legendary unchastity; something of the kind had occurred in India under Company rule.

5. Plaut. *Capt.* 68, *Cist.* 197, *Cas.* 87, Frank (1930), 71, n. 4.

6. *Machaera* (sword), *machina*, *catapulta*, *ballista* (siege-engine), *phylaca* (prison), *techina* (trick), Frank (1930), 70ff..

7. Frank (1930), 72, E. Fraenkel, *Elementi plautini in Plauto* (Firenze 1960), 149, n. 2, 183ff., 282, n. 1. E.g. *lautumiae* (quarry), *thermopolium* (cookshop), *anancaeum* (large drinking-vessel), *basilicus* (princely).

8. Kaimio (1979), 304ff., F. Leo, *Plautinische Forschungen* (2nd ed., Berlin 1912), 106, Middelmann (1938), J.-P. Cèbe, *Rev. Ét. Lat.* 38 (1960), 101ff., W.M. Seaman, *Class. Journ.* 50 (1954-5), 115ff., J.N. Hough, *Amer. Journ. Phil.* 56 (1925), 346ff.. T.J. Moore, *The theater of Plautus* (Austin 1998), 53ff. considers related issues. For Terence, cf. H. Haffter, *Terenzio e la sua personalità artistica* (Roma 1969), 70f. (in German, *Mus. Helv.* 10 (1953), 80f.).

9. Frank (1930), 70ff., Middelmann (1938), 40ff., E. Rawson, *Camb. Anc. Hist.* 8^2 (1989), 438, W.R. Chalmers in *Roman Drama* ed. T.R. Dorey and D.R. Dudley (London 1965), 39.

10. Cf. J. Kaimio, *Romans and the Greek language* (*Comm. human. litt.* 64, Helsinki 1979), 153ff.; for the Latin of soldiers stationed in Egypt, cf. J.N. Adams, *The vulgar Latin of the letters of Claudius Terentianus* (Manchester 1977), 2.

11. On immigrants and language, Noy (2000), 169ff. replaces earlier discussions.

12. See J. D'Arms, *Commerce and social standing in ancient Rome* (Cambridge, Mass. 1981), 24ff., 162ff. (fascinating).

13. Rawson (1985), 12, 22, Kaimio (1979), 36, 145, 216, Horsfall (1993), 814.

14. J. Andreau, *Mém. Ec. Fr. Rome (Ant.)* 80 (1968), 461ff.; note (e.g.) *danista* (moneylender), *symbola* (contributions to a common meal), *tocullio* (usurer), *teloneum* (customs post).

15. Cf. Middelmann (1938), 35ff., J. Hatzfeld, *Les trafiquants italiens* (Paris 1919), 333ff., W. Hilgers, *Lat. Gefässnamen* (Düsseldorf 1969).

16. *Bull. John Rylands Libr.* 59 (1977), 366. John Bodel, *Harv. Stud. Class. Phil.* 92 (1989), 349ff. notes *thymatulum* as a sausage-name (from the Greek word for *thyme*, the prime ingedient), much confused by our editions, usually as *tomacula* (as though 'links').

17. Mouritsen (2001), 133 offers a summary of recent statements.
18. Liv. 45.34.5; cf. Toynbee (*cit.* n. 1), 2, 171ff., T. Frank, *Economic survey of ancient Rome* 1 (Baltimore 1933), 67, 187f..
19. R. MacMullen in S.J.D. Cohen and E.S. Frerichs, *Diasporas in antiquity* (Atlanta 1993), 47ff. is queried in Noy (2000), 151f. (and cf. *id.*, 169ff. for immigration and language).
20. Cf. T. De Mauro, *Storia linguistica dell' Italia unita* (Bari 1986), 151 for dialect and the movement to Rome since WW2.
21. Cf. my remarks, Horsfall (1991), 63.
22. The phrasing in Seneca's, *Epist.* 26.2.
23. Horsfall (1993), 806f., S. Treggiari, *Roman freedmen* (Oxford 1969), *ead.*, *Papers Brit. School Rome* 43 (1975), 48ff..
24. Kaimio (1979), 192ff., Griffin (1985), 1ff..
25. F.T. Cooper, *Word-formation in the Roman sermo plebeius* (Boston 1895), 315ff., G. Bonfante, *Aufstieg und Niedergang* 2.29.1 (Berlin 1983), 436ff. = *Scritti scelti* 2 (Torino 1987), 612ff., Horsfall (1989), 77f..
26. Kaimio (1979), 301, 322, R.D. Brown, *Lucretius on love and sex* (Leiden 1987).
27. Cf. now D.R. Langslow, *Medical Latin in the Roman empire* (Oxford 2000), 76ff..
28. C. De Meo, *Lingue tecniche del Latino* (Bologna 1983), 50ff., R. Till, *La lingua di Catone* (Ital. tr., Roma 1968), indices ss.vv. *Grecismi, Greco*, S. Boscherini *Lingua e scienza greca nel 'De agri cultura' di Catone* (Roma 1970).
29. That is, of course, the Latin of the *vulgus*, or common people.
30. A.K. Bowman, J.D. Thomas, *Vindolanda: the Latin writing tablets* (Britannia Monographs 4, 1983), *iid.*, *The Vindolanda writing tablets* (London 1994), A.K. Bowman, *Life and letters on the Roman frontier* (London 1994), J.N. Adams, *Journ. Rom. Stud.* 85 (1995), 86ff.. For Bu Njem, see R. Marichal, *Les ostraka de Bu Njem, Libya antiqua* Suppl. 7, 1992, J.N. Adams, *Journ. Rom. Stud.* 84 (1994), 87ff.. See too Kaimio (1979), 153f..
31. La Graufesenque: R. Marichal, *Gallia*, Suppl. 47 (1988), 57ff.; for Magdalensberg, I collected some (German) bibliography at (1991), 68.
32. V. Väänänen, *Le Latin vulgaire des inscriptions pompéiennes* (Helsinki 1937), 187ff.; since 1937, we now have *CIL* 4.3, containing hundreds more graffiti, alas unindexed, but the overall picture is not changed.
33. Horsfall (1989), 74, M.W. Frederiksen, *Campania* (London

1984), 324, D'Arms (*cit.* n. 12), 105f. (and 97ff. for the 'typicality' of Trimalchio). Alternative locations for Trimalchio and dates for Petronius are still occasionally proposed by the loopy fringe.
34. Cf. Horsfall (1989), 77, with bibliography.
35. Tac. *Ann.* 15.33.
36. Strab. 5.4.7; cf. the ample discussion by John D'Arms, *Romans on the Bay of Naples* (Cambridge, Mass. 1970), 142ff..
37. Horsfall (1993), 798ff., Bonfante (*cit.* n. 25). The comic poet (in Plautus' time) Titinius (frag. 85, Ribbeck) remarks that the people of Ferentinum are keen on things Greek: in a little town between Anagni and Frosinone, an hour's drive ESE of Rome, the phenomenon is rather remarkable, and Ferentino can hardly have been some isolated freak! Cicero describes Italy in the years 100-90 BC as 'full of Greek arts and crafts' (more indeed, he goes on, than at Rome, *Arch.* 5). Cf. Wiseman (1987), 299.
38. For Aramaic, cf. Horsfall (1989), 86, n. 30. The analogy between the Greek of Rome and the Yiddish of New York is strikingly attractive: see Mencken (*cit.* n. 3), 633ff..
39. Cf. N.B. Crowther, *Ant. Class.* 52 (1983), 268ff., Balsdon (1969), 324ff..
40. Plut. *Mar.* 2.2, Cic. *Fam.* 7.1.3, *Att.* 16.5.1, Nic. Dam. *Vit. Caes.* 9.19, *Inscr. Lat. Sel.* 5050.157, 160f., 5052 (the Augustan *ludi saeculares*), J. Beaujeu in *Hommages H. Le Bonniec* (*Coll. Latom.* 201, Brussels 1988), 10ff..
41. Suet. *Caes.* 39.1 (by *vici*, quarters), *Aug.* 43.1 (by *regiones*).
42. See Rawson (1985), 22, 29, *ead.* (1991), 475ff., *ead.*, *Cambr. Anc. Hist.* 8^2 (1989), 469, Horsfall (1993), 803, Kaimio (1979), 215f. and still G. Michaut, *Sur les tréteaux latins* (Paris 1912), 251ff..
43. *Inscr. Lat. Sel.* 5213.11 = *Carm. Lat. Epigr.* 55.11.
44. Cic. *Fam.* 7.1.3 with Rawson (1991), 476.
45. Cic. *Tusc. Disp.* 2.7, Rawson (1985), 49, 53, Horsfall (1993), 799f..
46. Cic. *Fam.* 15.19.1.
47. Rawson (1985), 53, R. MacMullen, *Enemies of the Roman order* (Cambridge, Mass. 1975), 59ff., S. Dill, *Roman society from Nero to Marcus Aurelius* (repr. New York 1956), 334ff..
48. Rawson (1991), 570ff., *ead.* in *Tria lustra* (*Essays ... John Pinsent*) (Liverpool 1993), 255ff. (260: Pythagoreanism; cf. too *ead.* (1985), 53), Wiseman (1985), 28ff., Giancotti (1967), 119ff..
49. Horsfall (1989), 199f., with discussion and bibliography, F.R.D. Goodyear on *Copa* 37, *Bull. Inst. Class. Stud.* 24 (1977),

117ff., Cupaiuolo (1993), 18, C. Salles, *Lire à Roma* (Paris 1992) is on the right track, 192ff..
50. See Friedlaender, *SG* 2, 224f., Mayor on Juv. 1.17 *ubique*!
51. See L. Gamberale, *Riv. Fil.* 116 (1988), 489ff., G. Cavallo in *Princeps Urbium* (Milano 1991), 204, G. Susini in *Lo spazio letterario di Roma antica* (ed. G. Cavallo, etc.) 2 (Roma 1989), 271ff.. Discussions in English are lacking.
52. Cf. Mart. 3.44.11 for the latrine and see now R. Neudecker, *Die Pracht der Latrinen* (München 1994), 28.
53. See above, p. 65f..
54. Horsfall (1989), 80, R.J. Starr, *Latomus* 46 (1987), 199f., C.P. Jones in *Dining in a classical context*, ed. W.J. Slater (Ann Arbor 1991), 189.
55. Horsfall (1989), 79, A. Hardie, *Statius and the Silvae* (Liverpool 1983), 83ff..
56. Horsfall (1989), 79, Cic. *Arch.* 18, Hardie (*cit.*), 76ff., Stat. *Silv.* 1 *praef.* 22f., etc.
57. Horsfall (1989), 79f., Jones, (*cit.* n. 54), R.J. Starr, *CJ* 86 (1990-1), 337ff..
58. Horsfall (1995), 17, 249 (some of the evidence is clearly unsound, but such readings are altogether credible).
59. Ch. 1, n. 30.
60. Horsfall (1995), 249f., Macr. 5.17.5, Suet. *Ner.* 54.
61. Gell. 18.5.2 (and cf. 16.10.1), L. Gamberale, *Riv. Fil.* 117 (1989), 49ff., R.J. Starr, *Rhein. Mus.* 132 (1989), 411f.. Puteoli: D'Arms (*cit.* n. 36), 146f., 152.
62. Not excavated so far: N. Purcell in Frederiksen (*cit.* n. 33), 353.
63. Ov. *Trist.* 2.519, 5.7.25, Wille (1967), 185, E. Fantham, *CW* 82 (1989), 159.
64. Juv. 7.82ff., Stat. *Silv.* 5.2.162, V. Tandoi, *Maia* 21 (1969), 103ff.. There may, though, be a problem in Statius' use of *cunei*, 'wedges' of seats, into which the tiny space of the *odeon* was not normally divided: cf. R. Meinel, *Das Odeion* (Frankfurt 1980), 37ff., G.C. Izenour, *Roofed theaters of classical antiquity* (New Haven 1992), *passim*, K. Coleman in Coulston-Dodge (2000), 243ff..
65. Evidence and bibliography surveyed, *Riv. Fil.* 121 (1993), 82f..
66. At *Flor.* 5, a comparable uncertainty, of *comoedia*/*philosophus*/mime/tightrope-walker, but clearly in the theatre. At *Flor.* 18,

the longer list, as cited; there, the words *lacunarium effulgentia* suggest the coffered roof of an enclosed auditorium or *odeion*. The two excerpts could very well derive from one single original. F.H. Sandbach, *Class. Quart.* 32 (1982), 135 claims with atypical imprudence that *Flor.* 18 actually proves that there were tightrope-walkers in the *theatre*. Cf. further p. 62.

67. Horsfall (1989), 89, n. 97, Wiedemann (1992), 24, 57, P. Sabbatini Tumolesi, *Gladiatorum paria* (Roma 1980).
68. J. Frayn, *Markets and fairs in Roman Italy* (Oxford 1993), 40.
69. At least W. Beare, *The Roman stage* (2nd ed., London 1955), 163 faces the problem.
70. M. Gigante, *Civiltà delle forme letterarie nell' antica Pompeii* (Napoli 1979), 113ff. R. Meiggs, *Roman Ostia* (2nd ed., Oxford 1973), 420ff..
71. Dio 75.8.2, Meiggs (*cit.* n. 70), 423f..
72. T.P. Wiseman, *Pap. Brit. School Rome* 48 (1980), 13 = Wiseman (1987), 183, Wiseman (1994), 33, Horsfall (1989), 84, 194f., A.D. Booth, *Greece and Rome* 27 (1980), 166ff., Scobie (1983), 11.
73. Plin. *Epist.* 4.7.6, Schol. Pers. 1.134 'I do not want the *circulatores* to read my poem: in the morning they recite the praetor's or consul's edict, at midday they perform trivial songs'.
74. See n. 72; the long paper by H. Blümner on travelling folk in antiquity, *Sitz. Bayer. Akad. Müchen* 1918.6, remains indispensable.
75. Sings: n. 73; tells a story/myth: p. 98; reads a book, *ib.*
76. Readers: R.J. Starr (*cit.* n. 57); *aretalogi*, p. 57.
77. But note the formal records of the first performance, the *didascalica*; cf. (e.g.) E. Fantham, *Roman literary culture* (Baltimore 1996), 43.
78. Rawson (1991) contains most of the preliminary writing for the book Elizabeth Rawson did not live to undertake.
79. Chalmers (1965), 29, Beare (*cit.* n. 69), 163f.. R.C. Beacham, *The Roman theatre and its audience* (London 1991) discusses other matters. Women: Cic. *Tusc. Disp.* 1.37 *mulierculae et pueri*, 'women [derogatory] and boys' (cf. Vitr. 5.3.1). Cf. Rawson (1991), 510ff.. Slaves were admitted grudgingly, Plaut. *Poen.* 23ff., Rawson (1991), 513. Of prices and tickets we know nothing.
80. Cf. N. Zagagi, *Tradition and originality in Plautus* (Göttingen 1980), 20ff., Fraenkel (*cit.* n. 7), 53ff., Middelmann (1938), 48ff..
81. Fraenkel (*cit.* n. 7), 88f..
82. For art, cf. p. 90ff..
83. Wright (1931), 4, Guillemin (1937), 12f., Balsdon (1969),

273. Battles: see Plaut. *Capt.* 63. Note also the unknown (?)*praetexta* on the same occasion, with infantry and cavalry, Cic. *Fam.* 7.1.2, Wright (1931), 73.
84. *Poetics*, ch. 6; cf. Appendix 2 of D.W. Lucas' commentary.
85. Cic. *Fam.* 7.1.2, Wright (1931), 10, 34, 55.
86. Against the conventional view (e.g. Nicolet (1976), 479ff., T.P. Wiseman, *New men in the Roman senate* (Oxford 1971), 159ff.), though, cf. Gruen (1992), 188ff.. Note, in Gruen's favour, the silence of the *Commentariolum Petitionis*: no explicit instructions to put of a couple of good plays if you want to win an election!
87. For the last flickers of traditional comedy, cf. *SHA Hadr.* 26.4, Apul. *Flor.* 18 *comoedus sermocinatur*, the comic actor makes a speech. See H.D. Jocelyn, *Bull. Inst. Class. Stud.* Suppl. 51 (1988), 57. Decline of the old plays: Jory (1987), 147, *id.*, *Bull. Inst. Class. Stud.* 28 (1981), 147ff., Jocelyn (*cit.*), 57ff., *id.* in *Homage to Horace* (ed. S.J. Harrison, Oxford 1995), 228ff., Griffin (1985), 198ff..
88. W.J. Slater, *Class. Ant.* 13 (1994), 121ff., M. Kleijwegt, *Act. class.* 37 (1994), 93f., Jory (*cit.* n. 87).
89. Cf. M.A. Cavallaro, *Spese e spettacoli* (Bonn 1984), 207, n. 45, Jory (*cit.* n. 87).
90. Friedlaender, *SG* 2, 126, Bonaria (1965), 169ff., Wille (1967), 342f..
91. Cf. Chapter 1, n. 35.
92. Jürgens (1972), 241f., Weismann (1972), 45.
93. Rawson (1991), 570ff..
94. Cf. Cic. *Off.* 1.97, *Tusc. Disp.* 1.37, Wright (1931), 32f.. So too in Seneca's time, *Ep. Mor.* 108.8.
95. Cf. Chapter 2, n. 35, Cic. *Sest.* 118 *universus populus*, Wright (1931), 57f., Rawson (1991), 572, citing Cic. *Fin.* 5.63, *Amic.* 24.
96. I. Mariotti, *Introduzione a Pacuvio* (Urbino 1960), 30ff., Pacuvius, ed. G. D'Anna (Roma 1967), 76, Pacuv. frag. 197 Ribbeck, Cic. *Tusc. Disp.* 1.106.
97. A possibility denied by Strab. 1.2.8; cf. 83ff. on the alleged 'stupidity' of the *plebs*.
98. Cf. Rawson (*cit.* n. 48) for a new, loftier view of the mime!
99. Cf. Gruen (1992), 210ff., Sandbach (*cit.* n. 66), 134ff..
100. Cf. Brink's note on Hor. *Epist.* 2.1.186.
101. Bears: cf. Blümner (*cit.* n. 72), 21ff. (with n. 153), G. Jennison, *Animals for show and pleasure* (Manchester 1937), s.v.. Tightrope-walkers: Blümner (*cit.* n. 72), 13.
102. Hor. *Epist.* 2.1.210, August. *Epist.* 120.5 (*Patr. Lat.* 33.454),

de divin. daem. 8 (= *Corp. Script. Eccl. Lat.* 41.606.9), Sandbach (*cit.* n. 66). Cf. 67; I there discuss the evidence of Apul. *Flor.* 5, 18 which does not necessarily apply to the theatre at all.
103. For Hor. and Ter., cf. (e.g.) Muecke's commentary to *Serm.* 2 (Warminster 1993) and my remarks in *Style and tradition: studies in honor of Wendell Clausen* (Stuttgart 1998), 52f..
104. Liv. 1.35.9, Cic. *Leg.* 2.38, Dion. Halic. 7.73.3, Suet. *Aug.* 45, *Calig.* 18. Augustus' interest in watching back-street brawlers perform I discuss in *Anc. Hist.* 29 (1997), 25ff..
105. K. Coleman in Coulston-Dodge (2000), 227f..
106. Duckworth (1952), 66, 68.
Addendum: see now J.N. Adams' majestic *Bilingualism and the Latin language* (Cambridge 2003).

5. Fun for all

1. Cf. Rawson (1991), 475ff., with older bibliography.
2. Cf. L. Gamberale, *Riv. Fil.* 116 (1988), 489ff..
3. H. Solin in *Pompeii 79* (ed. F. Zevi, Napoli 1979), 278ff., V. Väänänen, *Recherches et recréations latino-romanes* (Napoli 1981), 73ff..
4. P. Cugusi, *Aspetti letterari dei CLE* (Bologna 1985), 22ff., Gamberale (*cit.* n. 2).
5. Cugusi (*cit.* n. 3), 91ff.
6. Cf. E. Champlin, *Final judgements* (Berkeley 1991), 70f..
7. Cupaiuolo (1993), 138f..
8. Cf. Petron. 58.8 (p. 81), Plaut. *Men.* 402ff., and *ib.* for the importance of riddles in general.
9. Cf. Tosi, n°766 (Cic. *Fam.* 7.3.4), n°553 (Cic. *Att.* 5.15.3), n°483 (Aulus Gellius *Praef.*19); cf. the children's song *rex erit* ..., p. 46, Sedgwick, Fraenkel (both *cit.* n. 10).
10. Wille (1967), 149, W.B. Sedgwick, *Greece and Rome* 1 (1932), 99f., E. Fraenkel, *Kleine Beiträge* 2 (Roma 1964), 18f., Courtney (1993), 470ff..
11. Cf. J. Fentress, C. Wickham, *Social memory* (Oxford 1992), 45ff..
12. A chapter-title in M. Beard, M. Crawford, *Rome in the late republic* (London 1985).
13. Harris (1989), 227 (cf. 14, 335); see Horsfall (1991), 72.
14. Rawson (1985), 50.
15. E. Rawson, *Camb. Anc. Hist.* 8^2 (1989), 438, R. MacMullen,

Historia 40 (1991), 428, M.H. Crawford in *Imperialism in the ancient world*, ed. P.D.A. Garnsey, etc. (Cambridge 1978), 200 etc..
   16. Cf. H.D. Jocelyn, *Bull. John Rylands Libr.* 59 (1977), 366, Horsfall (1989), (1991), (1993), Rawson in *Tria lustra (Essays ... John Pinsent)* (Liverpool 1993).
   17. Wiseman (1994), 33. The admirable W.G. Hoskins remarked in a broadcast 'most English historians are snobs'; see V. Neuburg, *Popular literature* (Harmondsworth 1977), 237ff.
   18. See p. 72ff..
   19. Cf. Citroni (1995), 16, 20, Rawson (1985), 49, Horsfall (1991), 63.
   20. S. Goldberg, *Epic in republican Rome* (Oxford 1995), 47f. has not upset S. Mariotti's work (in Italian) on the complex, Greek-influenced idiom of both (cf. G.B. Conte, *Latin literature* (Baltimore 1999), 45).
   21. Suet. *Caes.* 73.1 talks of the 'permanent branding' inflicted on Mamurra by Catullus.
   22. Cf. Purcell (1995), 35, R. Hoggart, *Uses of literacy* (Harmondsworth repr. 1984), 244f..
   23. Cf. Rawson (1991), 508ff., K. Coleman in Coulston-Dodge (2000), 231ff., H. Parker in Bergmann-Kondoleon (1999), 164. Until quite recently, you travelled first, second or third class on a British train, but all frequented the same bookstalls (and all classes bought the Pink 'Un, naturally): Neuburg (*cit. n.* 17), 200, J. Richards and J.M. Mackenzie, *The railway station: a social history* (Oxford 1988), 298ff.. Cf. further p. 100 for the illusion of cricket as part of a 'common ground'.
   24. Suet. *Aug.* 45.1 *ad spectandum*, not precise; cf. 53.1. Amply discussed, Millar (1977), 370f., Yavetz (1988), 100f..
   25. Note p. 112f. for Hadrian; cf. too Suet. *Tit.* 8.2, Balsdon (1969), 28, K. Coleman, *Classics Ireland* 8 (2001), 130, G.G. Fagan, *Bathing in public* (Ann Arbor 1999), 190ff..
   26. F. Münzer, PW s.v. Licinius, n°72, Val. Max. 8.7.6, Kaimio (1979), 96, 111, 144, Gruen (1992), 249.
   27. Horsfall (1995), 63ff..
   28. Frank, 358ff., Horsfall, *Riv. Fil.* 119 (1991), 212, *id.* (1995), 95.
   29. Medicine: Galen 2.280K, accountancy, *Inscr. Lat. Sel.* 7755, shorthand, *Pap. Oxy.* 4.724, farming, veterinary medicine: Horsfall (1995), 95, Colum. 1.1.3, etc.; architecture: Vitr. 1.1.4, etc.; law: Petr. 46.7, F. Schulz, *History of Roman legal science* (Oxford 1946), 156. See too Horsfall (1991), 63f..

30. Horsfall (1989), 77, 200, (1993), 799, Otto (1965), xv-xviii. For the use of proverbial expressions, cf. Plut. *Cat. Mai.* 8, Suet. *Aug.* 25, *Tib.* 25, *Vesp.* 16, *Domit.* 3.
31. Cf. Smith on Petr. 44.7, Horsfall (1989), 84; a 'finger-flashing' game.
32. For the long survival of local accents in the English aristocracy, cf. J. Honey, *Does accent matter?* (London 1989), 46. For Italy, cf. T. De Mauro, *Storia linguistica dell' Italia unita* (Bari 1986), 358.
33. Rawson (1985), 53, Horsfall (1993), 800, Giancotti (1967), 119ff., Wiseman (1994), 80. A fragment of Cicero, *Pro Gallio* (Cic. *orat. dep.* frag. 6.2) quoted by St Jerome, *Epist.* 52.8.3 (*Corp. Scr. Eccl. Lat.* 54, 1910).
34. Suet. *Tib.* 42.
35. H. Bardon, *Les empereurs et les letters latines* (Paris 1968) is less rewarding than the text of Suetonius; for Augustus, cf. *Ancient History* 27 (1997), 25ff. (cf. p. 78). For the emperor as giving a cultural/intellectual lead, cf. Plin. *Paneg.* 46.4, 54.1, M. Billerbeck, *Greece and Rome* 37 (1990), 191ff..
36. *Persa* 392ff. (Corbett (1986), 24); cf. *Stichus* 218ff. (Gelasimus hesitates whether to sell off his joke-books), Corbett (1986), 42.
37. Cf. Rawson (1985), 50f., Citroni (1995), 20, Scobie (1983), 14.
38. Much illumination in Corbett (1986).
39. Corbett (1986), 59, Ramage (1973), 72, Opelt (1967), index s.v. *scurra*.
40. Cf. my note (Venosa 1993) on Hor. *Epist.* 1.7.56. Corbett (1986), 60.
41. Cic. *De orat.* 2.253, Corbett (1986), 60ff., Ramage (1973), 78f., Courtney (1993), 475, H. Haffter, *Römische Politik und römische Politiker* (Heidelberg 1967), 145ff..
42. Corbett (1986), 66, Cupaiuolo (1993), 53f., O. Skutsch in *Studies in honour of T.B.L. Webster* ed. J.H. Betts, etc. 1 (Bristol 1987), 223f..
43. See I.M. Le M. Du Quesnay in *Poetry and politics in the age of Augustus* (ed. T. Woodman, D. West, Cambridge 1984), 19ff..
44. Horsfall (1989); Maria Plaza, *Laughter and derision in Petronius' Satyrica* (Stockholm 2000), 84ff. has explored the issue with subtlety and I am delighted to have been able to discuss Petronius with her.
45. Horsfall (1989), 83.
46. Cf. Horsfall (1989), 80, 83ff., C.P. Jones in *Dining in a*

Notes to pages 72-76

classical context, ed. W.J. Slater (Ann Arbor 1991), 190f., R.J. Starr, *Latomus* 46 (1987), 199f..
47. Cf. R. Nauta, *Poetry for patrons* (Leiden 2002), 142ff., Jones (*cit*. n. 46), 185ff., Horsfall (1989), 79f.; see too D. Hershkowitz, *Greece and Rome* 42 (1995), 168ff., A.D. Vardi, *Scr. Class. Isr.* 21 (2002), 83ff., A.-M. Guillemin, *Pline et la vie littéraire de son temps* (Paris 1929). Jones and I (1989, 87, nn. 53, 61) unearthed simultaneously (or nearly so) the importance of Plut. *Quaest. conv.* 711A, dramatic performances of Platonic dialogues after dinner. But here the challenge to Roman bilingualism seems a little fierce or unrealistic and Plutarch may have Greek usage more clearly in mind.
48. Jones (*cit*. n. 46), Horsfall (1989), 80f., Blümner (1918), 6f., Starr (*cit*. n. 46).

6. To help pass the time

1. Cf. Horsfall (1989), 85, 209, H.A. Harris, *Sport in Greece and Rome* (London 1972), 223ff..
2. Cic. *De orat.* 2.239, 259, etc., Wright (1931), 53f., L. Desmouliez, *Cicéron et le goût* (*Coll. Lat.* 150, Bruxelles 1976), 301.
3. Caesar: Gellius 17.14.1, Macrob. 2.3.10; the younger Cato: Val. Max. 2.10.8; Sulla: Plut. *Sull.* 36.1 *et passim*; Antony: Plut. *Ant.* 9.6.
4. Hor. *Serm.* 2.6.44, where Muecke well draws attention to Cic. *Fam.* 2.8.1, where Cicero reproves Caelius for sending him news of the matching of gladiators.
5. Petr. 45.5-8.
6. Epict. 3.16.4.
7. Cf. 70.13 for betting at the races.
8. Pompeii, Horsfall (1989), 89, n. 97, B. Kellum in Bergmann-Kondoleon (1999), 287; Magdalensberg, Horsfall (1991), 68.
9. Cf. n. 1; Balsdon (1969) knew virtually all the evidence, but his outlook was still essentially senatorial, and the idea of *shared* pleasures would, I fear, have shocked him.
10. Väterlein (1976), 110, s.v. *pila*; Trimalchio: Petr. 27; Caesar: Macr. 2.6.5; Pliny: *Epist.* 2.17.12; Cicero (?): *De fato* 34, Väterlein, 94f.; Augustus: Suet. *Aug.* 83; Cato: Sen. *Epist. Mor.* 104.33, Sex. Titius (*trib. pleb.*): Cic. *De orat.* 2.253, 3.88; Vestricius Spurinna: Plin. *Epist.* 3.1.8 (a very distinguished friend of P.); Piso: *Laus Pisonis* 183ff. (wonderful account of how a young noble is reduced to

passing his days; cf. E. Champlin, *Mus. Helv.* 46 (1989), 101ff.); Urso: *Inscr. Lat. Sel.* 5173 (AD 126).
11. Väterlein (*cit.* n. 10), Balsdon (1969), 163ff..
12. R.G. Austin, *Greece and Rome* 4 (1934), 26-34, 76-82, G. Montesano, *Dizionario epigrafico* 4 (Roma 1964-85), 2240f.; cf. Horsfall, *Bull. Inst. Class. Stud.* 30 (1983), 96, n. 17. On *Laus Pis.* (*cit.* n. 10), cf. J. Richmond, *Mus. Helv.* 51 (1994), 164ff., against Purcell (1995), 16. It is singular that Huizinga, in *Homo ludens*, starts from a profoundly partial view of the 'ludic element' in Roman life; ch. 11 is a remarkable accumulation of misinformed prejudices. See Purcell (1995), 19, n. 70 and 30, n. 112 for *Inscr. Lat. Sel.* 7755a, the epitaph of an artist in the art (of making/playing? Not clear) board counters.
13. Cf. Seneca, *Epist. Mor.* 56.1 for gamblers in an urban context (with Purcell (1995), 17ff.).
14. G. Barbieri, G. Montesano, *Dizionario epigrafico* (*cit.* n. 12), 2230ff., Purcell (*cit.* n. 12), 18, n. 69, Horsfall, *Bull. Inst. Class. Stud.* 30 (1983), 96, n. 17. Manhandling, *ib.*, 86.
15. The Cross, p. 114; the Wall: R.W. Davies, *Aufstieg und Niedergang* ... 2.1 (Berlin 1974), 332 = *Service in the Roman army* (Edinburgh 1989), 67. Taverns: *Copa* 37, Purcell (1995), 27, Kleberg (1957), 118.
16. Cf. Opelt (1965), 157, 159, Cic. *Cat.* 2.10, 23, *Phil.* 13.24, Shackleton Bailey on *Att.* 14.5.1, Suet. *Aug.* 71, with Horsfall, *Ancient History* 27 (1997), 27, Purcell (1995), 13f., *Calig.* 41.2, *Nero* 22, *Vitell.* 4, *Claud.* 33.2 (cf. Sen. *Apoc.* 12). Cf. Väterlein (1976), 37f.. Roman betting in general is much neglected: cf. T. Mommsen, *Römisches Strafrecht* (Leipzig 1889), 860f..
17. Cf. Juv. 3.278ff., Balsdon (1969), 154, E. Eyben, *Restless youth* (London 1993), 107ff.. Cicero reproached his political enemies with frequenting low hostelries: *Pis.* 13, 18, Opelt (1965), 158, Kleberg (1957), 93; see too Lucilius 11 (Marx's numbering), Suet. *Gramm.* 15, Vitell. 7, 13.
18. Cf. Courtney's note on Juv. 5.171, Horsfall, *La villa sabina di Orazio* (Venosa 1993), 93, J.H. D'Arms in *Sympotica* (ed. O. Murray, Oxford 1990), 308ff..
19. Cf. Suet. *Aug.* 74.1, Plin. *Epist.* 2.6, *Paneg.* 49.4ff., Juv. 8.171-6, with the commentaries; D'Arms (*cit.* n. 18) is exceptionally illuminating. At *Laus Pis.* 126 praise is offered simply for the lack of spiteful motives in the inviting of guests.

20. Cf. my commentary on Nepos, *Atticus* 13.3 (Oxford 1989), *Greece and Rome* 42 (1995), 49ff., Citroni (1995), 9.
21. Cf. Horsfall, *Ancient History* 27 (1997), 25ff..
22. *Ib.*, 26f. on Suet. *Aug.* 83.1.
23. Cf. Suet. *Aug.* 45.2, 71, 74.2, 78, 83.1; cf. n. 21. Had Augustus actually in mind Caesar's desire to be seen to be a friend of the people? Yavetz (1988), 51.
24. Cf. August. *De civ. Dei* 18.18 'in the books which Apuleius entitled "Golden Ass" '; see too Lucr. 3.12f., Cic. *Acad.* 2.119. See A. Scobie, *Rhein. Mus.* 122 (1979), 239.
25. The classic, recognisably Homeric antithesis of bronze and gold, *Iliad* 6.236.
26. Plin. *Epist.* 9.33.2.
27. Cf. Trenkner (*cit.* n. 33), 68, A. Stramaglia, *Zeitschr. Pap. Epigr.* 84 (1990), 19ff., and *id.*, *Res inauditae, incredulae* (Bari 1999).
28. Plin. *Epist.* 7.27.1, with Stramaglia (*cit.* n. 27 (1999)), 144ff..
29. Adams (1982), 1ff., 214ff..
30. *Ib.*, 214.
31. Suet. *Tib.* 43.2.
32. Theodore Priscian *Logicus* 11.34; cf. Horsfall, *Scr. Class. Isr.* 11 (1991-2), 135.
33. Plut. *Crass.* 32, S. Trenkner, *The Greek novella* (Cambridge 1958), 172ff., Rawson (1991), 369f..
34. Val. Max. 2.10.8, Sen. *Epist. Mor.* 97.8; the crowd would not call for the last stitch to be removed while Cato the younger was present, so he was graciously pleased to withdraw, eventually!
35. Jürgens (1972), 86, n. 2, 233, n. 4, R.W. Reynolds, *Class. Quart.* 40 (1946), 80. The bed: Ps.-John Chrysostom, *Patr. Graec.* 56.543. Sexual acts: *SHA Elag.* 25.4; cf. Minuc. Felix 37.12, Val. Max. 2.6.7. See p. 128.
36. Adams (1982), 219.
37. *Journ. Rom. Stud.* 71 (1981), 50ff., and in *Sources for ancient history* (ed. M. Crawford, Cambridge 1983), 1ff..
38. Werewolf: Petr. 61.6ff., witches, 63.2ff., ephebe of Pergamum, 85-6, widow of Ephesus, 110-12. Neglected in recent work on Petronius; see though O. Pecere, *La novella della matrona di Efeso* (Padova 1975), *I racconti del 'Satyricon'*, ed. P. Fedeli, R. Dimundo (Roma 1988), *Semiotica della novella latina* (Roma 1986).
39. Petr. 51, Plin. *Nat.* 36.195, Cassius Dio 57.21, C. Santini in *Semiotica* (*cit.* n. 38), 117ff..
40. Otto (1965), Tosi (1991), M.C. Sutphen, *A collection of Latin*

proverbs supplementing Otto (Baltimore 1902), R. Häussler, *Nachträge zu A. Otto* ... (Hildesheim 1968).
41. For Petronius, cf. Horsfall (1989), 76f.; Augustus: Suet. *Aug.* 87; cf. *Tib.* 59, *Calig.* 30. When Caesar remarked that the die was cast (*alea iacta est*), he was quoting Menander (frag. 59.4K-Th., and Suetonius' Latin simplifies the Greek, which refers to a die already cast, not to one about to be!) but the number of variations on the remark suggest that cast dice soon became a proverb, more than a quotation, Tosi (1991), n°1609.
42. Scobie (1983), 16ff..
43. Quint. 1.10.32, Tac. *Dial.* 29, Scobie (1983), 17ff.; cf. Cic. *Leg.* 1.57.
44. K. Ziegler, PW s.v. *Ploutarchos*, 21 (1951), 886.23ff. and see Theodorsson's commentary (Göteborg 1990) on Plut. *cit..*
45. How you get from Gk. *kaisara* to 666: see Horsfall (1989), 88, n. 80, *Class. Quart.* 24 (1974), 111. Such *gematria* is conventionally Greek, not Roman, alas.
46. Petr. 58.8 with Smith's n., W. Schultz PW s.v. *Rätsel*, 1A (1914), 116.16ff., Pompeii: *Corp. Inscr. Lat.* 4.1877, proverbs: Otto (1965), xxv.
47. Verg. *Buc.* 3.104ff., Liv. 1.54.6, 56.12.
48. At school: see Quint. 1.9.2, Bonner (1977), 253ff., Otto (1965), xxvii; fables in Enn. *Sat.*, frr. 21-58 of Vahlen's ed.; see too Lucilius 988 (Marx's numbering); widespread in Horace; see e.g. my note on *Epist.* 1.7.29-39.
49. Phaedr. 3, prol. 34ff.; W. Hansen, *An anthology of Greek popular literature* (Bloomington 1998), 106ff. reprints L.W. Daly's translation of one of the ancient versions of the *Life of Aesop*, an immensely popular ancient novel, on which cf. K. Hopkins, *Past and Present* 138 (1993), 3ff. (in particular 13, n. 18).
50. Cf. Harris (1989), 228, Citroni (1995), 20, Horsfall (1991), 72, Quint. 1.8.19, 9.1f..

7. Hypocrisy and evidence: the case of Cicero

1. The slanders (mingled with fair criticisms!) of J. Carcopino, *Les secrets de la correspondance de Cicéron* (2 vols, Paris 1947) remain unmatched.
2. Wright (1931), 24 (see even the letter Cic. *Fam.* 15.6.1), W.A. Laidlaw in *Studies in Cicero* (Roma 1962), 129ff. ('I even learned the sculptors' names', *Verr.* 2.4.4, *didici etiam ... artificum nomina!*). Cf.

Nisbet on Cic. *Pis.* 68; further bibliography collected, *Pap. Leeds Lat. Sem.* 7 (1993), 7, n. 36.

3. *Sest.* 119 (e.g.), Wright (1931), 24f.. Cf. A.E. Astin, *Cato the Censor* (Oxford 1978), 179, C. Edwards, *The politics of immorality* (Cambridge 1993), 98ff..

4. *De orat.* 3.83, 214, etc., Wright (1931), 26ff., Edwards (*cit.* n. 3), 117ff..

5. Wright (1931), 31ff., E. Malcovati, *Cicerone e la poesia* (Pavia 1943), 20ff..

6. Cf. pp. 26, 93f..

7. Cf. Cic. *Sest.* 97 (even businessmen and freedmen can be *optimates*; cf. C. Wirszubski, *Journ. Rom. Stud.* 44 (1954), 7 = Seager (1969), 189), 108 (the *verus populus*!), 138 ('of whatever order'), *Leg. agr.* 2.70 *optimorum ciuium* ('excellent citizens'), with Millar (1998), 104; see too Yavetz (1988), 153, Hellegouarc'h (1963), 491 (plebeian *boni*), 514, 536ff.; everything dismissed by Mouritsen (2001), 141 as 'rhetorical genuflection' (but see too *ib.*, 14). *Leg. agr.* 2.70f. is rich in compliments upon the urban beneficiaries of Rullus' land-distribution. The *Comm. Pet.* speaks of plebeians *navos et gratiosos*, active and influential (§29); the text *may* be post-Ciceronian, but the detail is stunningly good and careful.

8. *Mur.* 61 *Et quoniam non est nobis haec oratio habenda aut in imperita multitudine aut in aliquo conventu agrestium audacius paullo de studiis humanitatis quae et mihi et vobis nota et iucunda sunt disputabo.*

9. I render *corona*, the 'crown', or innermost ring of interested bystanders crucial to any public speaking at Rome: cf. Wiseman (1985), 69, Taylor (1964), 99.

10. See Nisbet (*cit.* n. 2).

11. *quid, quod homines infima fortuna, nulla spe rerum gerendarum, opifices denique delectantur historia*? See C. Schulze in *Past Perspectives* ed. I.S. Moxon, etc. (Cambridge 1986), 134f..

12. Plin. *Nat.*, *praef.* 6; Citroni (1995), 46 fails to notice the subjunctive: he *could* have written for such a public.

13. Dion. Hal. *Thuc.* 50; see Schulze (*cit.* n. 11), 124ff., T.P. Wiseman, *History* 66 (1981), 386 = *Roman studies* (Liverpool 1987), 255.

14. At various levels: cf. p. 68f..

15. Appendix 2, p. 122ff. on moral saws in Castricius' inscription and Quint. 5.11.19 for fairy-stories; cf. further p. 81.

16. Plin. *Epist.* 5.6.6 (reminiscences), 8.8.7 (graffiti), 7.30.3, 9.15.1, 36.6 (petitions).
17. *Orator* 168, *De orat.* 3.198. Guillemin (1937), 14 did very well to note the importance of these texts. Cf. too Dupont (1985), 115f..
18. *Orator* 173; cf. *De orat.* 3.98, 198.
19. *Ut non desideres planius dici*, Cic. *De orat.* 3.50; cf. Guillemin (1937), 15. Let us not forget the petitions presented to Pliny (see n. 16). See Brunt (1988), 372ff. for the *patronus* and the client's legal business.
20. Cf. Cic. *Sest.* 115ff., *Vatin.* 31; for the public banquet, cf. J. D'Arms, in Bergmann-Kondoleon (1999), 305f..
21. *De orat.* 1.221f., 2.153. Cf. below, p. 87, for orators and oratory suited to the *contio*.
22. Note *Tusc. Disp.* 2.3: oratory is a *popularis facultas*, a popular skill, in which the orator seeks to be approved by the judgement of the multitude – if the multitude be his audience in the first place.
23. Cf. Citroni (1995), 46ff. and (excellent) Guillemin (1937), 18ff..
24. As Cicero well knew, *De orat.* 2.25.
25. Cf. Rawson (1991), 570ff..
26. Cf. H.W. Litchfield, *Harv. Stud. Class. Phil.* 25 (1914), 1ff., M. Rambaud, *Cicéron et l'histoire* (Paris 1952), 25ff., W.M. Bloomer, *Valerius Maximus and the rhetoric of the new nobility* (London 1992), H. Kornhardt, *Exemplum* (diss. Göttingen 1936).
27. Cf. n. 39; add Rambaud (*cit.* n. 26), 36ff., D. Mack, *Senatsreden und Volksreden bei Cicero* (diss. Kiel 1937), 77.
28. Cf. Millar (1998), 95f..
29. See the commentary by W.B. Tyrrell (Amsterdam 1978).
30. See Nippel (1995), 34, Millar (1998), 59f., 95ff., (2002), 180ff., Mouritsen (2001), 13f., 24f., 38ff., Nicolet (1976), 386ff., F. Pina Polo, *Klio* 77 (1995), 203ff., L.R. Taylor, *Roman Voting Assemblies* (Ann Arbor 1966), 15ff., 21ff., T. Mommsen *Römisches Staatsrecht* 3 (Leipzig 1887), 389ff..
31. Cf. Millar (1998), 38ff., (2002), 180f. (the *contio* complementary to discussion in the nearby Senate). The historical origin of the *Rostra* known to a *contio*, *Leg. Man.* 55.
32. Cf. Mouritsen (2001), 39ff. (judicious). The make-up of the crowd was different, surely, on each occasion (cf. p. 26ff.) and though we do not exactly who came, and how they managed, Cicero's letters do demonstrate the important fact: many actually came.

33. Cf. Cic. *Att.* 1.16.11, *Verr.* 1.45; a full discussion, Mouritsen (2001), 47f. and see Millar (1998), 64f..
34. Cf. Mouritsen (2001), 25, M.H. Hansen, *Historia* 42 (1993), 161ff. I have discussed the question of audibility with both Prof. Hansen and Prof. Millar and would say more, were there (yet) any clear answer.
35. Cf. Pina Polo (n. 30), 205, Mouritsen (2001), 53f., Millar (1998), 60, (2002), 163, 180f.. See for example Plut. *Pomp.* 51, Cic. *Sest.* 126, *Mil.* 8 and above all, *QFr.* 2.3.2. For the whole range of the functions of *contiones*, see Vanderbroeck (1987), 209ff., Pina Polo (n. 30), 207ff..
36. So, notably, Cic. *de orat.* 2.338 *ut ... maxima quasi oratoris scaena uideatur contionis* (cf. *Ad Brut.* 1.9.2, a proverbial stage, as Hor. *Sat.* 2.1.71); see Guillemin (1937), 10, H.C. Gotoff, *Harv. Stud. Class. Phil* 95 (1993), 292f., Powell on Cic. *Amic.* 97. *Theatrum* is also so used, less strikingly, more commonly.
37. See M.Gleason, *Making men* (Princeton 1993), 103ff..
38. Cicero wrote of his own *Pro Rabirio omni genere amplificationis exarsimus* (*Orator* 102): 'I blazed out with every kind of enlargement'. See further Cic. *Brutus* 85f., 114, *De orat.* 2.338, 3.211 (the rare ability to master a *contio*). Cf. Guillemin (1937), 11.
39. A. Vasaly, *Representations* (Berkeley 1993).
40. *Ex memoria vestra ac patrum vestrorum*, *Rab. Perd.* 15. On the duration of popular historical memory at Athens, cf. Thomas (1989), 95ff.; the discussion of Rome in Thomas (1992), 158ff. is by comparison rather disappointing. For more recent times, see J. Fentress and C. Wickham, *Social memory* (Oxford 1992), 92ff..
41. See Appendix B (A), p. 94.
42. Cf. E.S. Gruen, *Last generation of the Roman republic* (repr. Berkeley 1995), 278 for the whole business of judicial antiquarianism (and cf. 78f. for the politics of the trial).
43. See *Rab. Perd.* 20ff..
44. See Appendix B (B), p. 94f..
45. Cf. E.R. Mix, *Marcus Atilius Regulus. Exemplum historicum* (The Hague 1970) for just one case-study.
46. See already *Class. Rev.* 39 (1989), 229.
47. Cf. the contributions of J. von Ungern-Sternberg and D. Timpe to *Vergangenheit in mündlicher Überlieferung* ed. J.v.U-S. and H. Reinau (Stuttgart 1988). A proper caution, T.J. Cornell, *Beginnings of Rome* (London 1995), 10ff..
48. I refer again to Mouritsen (2001), 36ff., 39ff. for careful

consideration of the competition of state and personal business for the *opifex*'s time.

49. See e.g. *Post red. in sen.* 25, 37, *Post red. ad Quir.* (the *contio* speech) 9, 11, J.-M. Claassen, *Displaced persons* (London 1999), 158ff..

50. Horsfall (1995), 148f..

51. Cf. (e.g.) *Pis.* 14, 58, *Sest.* 143, *Planc.* 60.

52. See e.g. *Verr.* 2.3.160.

53. E.g. *Rep.* 3.5.

54. Rawson (1985), 53, (cf. 266) perplexingly cites Cic. *Verr.* 2.4.126 as evidence for some consciousness on the Romans' part of the educative force of art on view (we might also consider Aristides *Orat. Rom.* (26 Keil) 13 on Rome as a sort of museum of international art). Cicero, though is here only concerned with the accessibility of art on view in Rome, not with its didactic importance. But note too Strabo 1.2.3 on the deterrent moral effect of certain mythological scenes. On reading inscriptions out loud, cf. Ennius *Scipio*, in *Varia* 2 with D.S. Potter, *Literary texts and the Roman historian* (London 1999), 108.

55. Cf. (e.g.) T. Hölscher, *Staatsdenkmal und Publikum* (Konstanz 1984), P.J. Holliday, *The origins of Roman historical commemoration in the visual arts* (Cambridge 2002) and E. Zinserling in *Sozialökonomische Verhältnisse ...* (ed. H. Diesner, Berlin 1959), 346ff..

56. The point made by Aelius Aristides (n. 54); M. Pape, *Griechische Kunstwerke aus Kriegsbeute* (diss. Hamburg 1975) is indispensable.

57. Plin. *Nat.* 35.23; see T. Hölscher, in *Tainia R. Hampe dargebracht* 1 (Mainz 1980), 353, M. Torelli, *Typology and structure of Roman historical reliefs* (Ann Arbor 1982), 121.

58. App. *Civ.* 2.419.

59. Cf. I.S. Ryberg, *Rites of the state religion in Roman art* (Mem. Amer. Acad. Rome 22, 1955), 147, C. Barini, *Triumphalia* (Torino 1952), 15, R. Cagnat, DS 5.1, 489, W. Ehlers, PW *Realencyclopädie* 2.13 (1939), 503.16-23.

60. *Phil.* 6.13.

61. *Leg. agr.* 2.95. Destruction of Capua: *ib.* 2.87 and note theme of empires of the past, *Leg. Man.* 11, 54.

62. Cic. *Leg. agr.* 2.97 (with 1.20), *Pis.* 24, *post red. in sen.* 17.

63. Liv. 26.34.12.

64. Vell. 1.11.2-5, Plin. *Nat.* 34.31. With the list of wars, cf. that in *Leg. Man.* 14.

65. Plin. *Nat.* 34.32.
66. Cf. Petr. 58.7 *lapidarias litteras scio*, Horsfall (1991), 62.
67. Cf. Plin. *Nat.* 34.24, Cic. *Leg. Man.* 11.

8. Implications

1. Since B.G. Niebuhr, *Römische Geschichte*, first ed., 1812 (137ff. in the 1853 ed.), after Jacob Perizonius (1709): see H.J. Erasmus, *The origin of Rome in historiography from Petrarch to Perizonius* (Assen 1935), 116f.. For the debate since Niebuhr, cf. (e.g.) Wiseman (1998), 1f., 153f.. Macaulay's *Lays* were written to show what these *carmina* might have been.
2. Wiseman (1998), 14 seems to wriggle on the hook! Peter Wiseman and I have disagreed, violently, even, about the fragments of Roman myth and their transmission, but he has contributed prodigiously to our understanding of the historical culture of the Roman republic and the channels of its transmission. This is not the moment to offer a bibliographical tour of old battlefields and I sense that at *cit.*, 14 he feels the same.
3. Cf. H. Flower, *Class. Quart.* 45 (1995), 170ff., against Wiseman (1994), 1ff.; cf. now Wiseman (1998), 1ff. and P Kragelund, etc. in *Symb. Osl.* 77 (2002).
4. Cf. Horsfall, *Riv. Fil.* 122 (1994), 50ff. (at 70ff.: in English), against Wiseman (1998), 14.
5. Horsfall (*cit.* n. 4), 63ff..
6. See below, p. 5ff..
7. *Athen.* 66 (1988), 32ff. (in Italian).
8. Cf. further Fantham on Ov. *Fasti* 4.377-8, 689-90.
9. *Clarorum uirorum laudes atque uirtutes*, Cat. *Orig.* frag. 118P.
10. Cf. Aristotle's ample use of them in *Ath. Pol.*; for Dicaearchus, cf. Horsfall (*cit.* n. 4), 70f.. The fragments of symposium-song collected, Page, *PMG*, p. 471ff..
11. Cf. Horsfall (1987), 1ff., Wiseman (nn. 1, 3), *passim*; we both give ample further references.
12. 'Performers from the Circus Maximus, whom I think we should imagine as strolling players', Wiseman (1994), 33. I translate Dio's words with care.
13. Cf. Mouritsen (2001), 2f..
14. Horsfall (1989), 74ff., 194ff..
15. Cf. H.D. Jocelyn, *Bull. John Rylands Libr.* 59 (1977), 366, E. Rawson in *Tria lustra (Essays ... John Pinsent)* (Liverpool 1993), 260.

16. In which the urban *plebs* was legendarily skilled; several instances have been cited in passing. Cf. Ramage (1973).
17. For violent political activity, cf. Lintott (1968), Nippel (1995), Vanderbroeck (1987), 146ff..
18. G.M. Trevelyan, *Social history* (London 1946), 408; quoted in R. Guha's engrossing *A corner of a foreign field* (London 2002), 52.
19. Cf. Bernard Ashmole, *An autobiography* (Oxford 1994), 76ff. for a long wartime plane journey in company far too unlikely for any fiction.
20. His hobbies studied, *Ancient history* 27 (1997), 25ff..
21. R. McKibbin, *Classes and cultures* (Oxford 2000), 527: 'England had no common culture'; cf. 94f. on sport.
22. Cf. Guha (*cit.* n. 17) pl. 11, p. 106, *et passim*, McKibbin (*cit.* n. 20), 335, D. Birley, *Social history of English cricket* (London 2000), 51.
23. Cf. Brunt (1971), 98f., 103: a date at which a major social upheaval would not have been unlikely.

Appendix 1

The Macquarie Ancient History Association gave swift and generous permission to reprint (with minor corrections) this article from *Ancient history* 29 (1999), 107-17.
1. I am most grateful for the reactions of audiences in Manchester, Rome, Lausanne, Venice, Groningen and Stockholm to versions of this paper, as well as to Ramsay MacMullen for inspiration and encouragement.
2. It was Giovanni Franco who led me to Tib. 1.10.31f.; his scholarship, conversation and hospitality lent a special enchantment to my visits to Venice. To him I express my thanks and to him this paper would naturally have been dedicated, were it not for the untimely death of Norman Austin (Massey), a very dear friend, and a modest, thoughtful (and sometimes loquacious) veteran of long years of counter-insurgency operations.
3. Cf. E.C. Evans, *Physiognomics in the ancient world* (Philadelphia 1969). A. Corbeill, *Controlling laughter* (Princeton 1996), 55f. (his forthcoming *Gesture in ancient Rome* contains a rich fund of further material).
4. Evans (*cit.* n. 3), 50f., 93f.: A. Wallace-Hadrill, *Suetonius* (London 1983), 67ff. misses the link. The *de physiognomonia liber*

(Budé ed. 1981, BUR ed. [Italian] 1993) really deserves to be much better known; I know of no English translation.
  5. Nostrils, Juv. 14.194; haircut, *ib.*; muscles, Cic. *Phil.* 8.26, Pers. 3.86; calves, Juv. 16.14; varicose veins, Pers. 5.189; hairy legs, Fronto 2, 148Haines (Loeb); hygiene, Pers. 3.77. For the uniformed soldier in Rome, cf. J. Coulston in Coulston-Dodge (2000), 91.
  6. On *Serm.* 1.6.73, cf. now G.W. Williams in *Homage to Horace* (Oxford 1995), 305.
  7. Veget. 2.14; perhaps even *c.* AD 5, but deeply conservative and derivative. Cf. N.P. Milner's trans. and comm., Liverpool 1993.
  8. *Tusc. Disp.* 4.55, *pugnaces*, *Phil.* 8.26.
  9. Cf. C. De Meo, *Lingue tecniche del latino* (Bologna 1983), 187ff., M.G. Mosci Sassi, *Il sermo castrensis* (Bologna 1983). Surprisingly little on the Vindolanda tablets.
  10. Cf. Juv. 8.174 with Mayor's note, Kleberg (1957), 92.
  11. *Vir. ill.* 24; cf. Sall. *Iug.* 85.29 ('not *imagines* but *cicatrices*'), Plu. *Cat. Mai.* 1 (body covered with scars even when young), Cic. *De orat.* 2.124, Sall. *Hist.* 1.88, Liv. 2.23.4, 6.20.8, Hor. *Carm.* 1.35.3, Sen. *Contr.* 1.8.3, Tac. *Ann.* 1.35.1, Plut. *Mar.* 9.2. Cf. G. Majno, *The healing hand* (Cambridge, Mass. 1979), 316f..
  12. *Civ.* 3.53.4; cf. Sall. *Hist.* 1.88, Tac. *Ann.* 2.9.2, Juv. 10.158 and the *cognomina* Luscus, Luscinus and Cocles.
  13. Plin. *Nat.* 7.104f. (on which, see Schilling's Budé commentary); cf. Juv. 3.48.
  14. Epict. 4.13.5: see N.J.E. Austin and N.B. Rankov, *Exploratio* (London 1995), 136f..
  15. Criminals in: MacMullen (n. 18, 1984/1990), n. 9; soldiers as thieves and bullies: Petr. 82, Juv. 16, Apul. *Met.* 9.39ff., Millar (*cit.* n. 16); veterans or deserters as bandits: Courtney on Juv. 16.9, B. .Shaw, *Past and Present* 105 (1984), 29f., K. Coleman, *European Review* 5.4 (1997), 405.
  16. MacMullen (1963), 77ff., F. Millar, *Journ. Rom. Stud.* 71 (1981), 67f., E. Courtney's introduction to Juv. 16 (London 1980).
  17. R. Alston, *Soldier and society in Roman Egypt* (London 1995), 6ff..
  18. *Historia* 33 (1984), 440ff. = *id.* (1990), 225ff., N. Pollard in *Journ. Rom. Arch.* Suppl. 18 (1996), 211ff..
  19. 'Legionary' first marched at Manchester University; I had just dined, fascinatingly, with a Guardsman's daughter and her ex-SAS husband; my special thanks to Valerie and Jeff, but numerous Eng-

lish, Australian, Russian, German, Israeli, Dutch, Swedish, Swiss, Italian, American, Rhodesian and Polish friends (and relatives) have contributed to my understanding of the naval/military anecdote.

20. P.A. Brunt, *Italian manpower* (Oxford 1971), 285ff..
21. J. Coulston in Coulston-Dodge (2000), 76ff., Nippel (1995), 90ff.; cf. MacMullen (1975), 164, 167ff., Millar (1977), 64.
22. Cf. Millar (*cit.* n. 21) and *Carm. Lat. Epigr.* 1320.
23. Cf. Sherwin-White on Plin. *Epist.* 10.37.3.
24. On Nonius Datus (*Corp. Inscr. Lat.* 8.2728 with 18122, *Inscr. Lat. Sel.* 5795) I have written at *Omnibus Omnibus* (1987), 40f. and *Bull. Inst. Class. Stud.* Suppl. 51 (1988), 54f.. See further p. 124ff. below.
25. 'Relatively little fear of bandits' wrote L. Casson, ingenuously (*Travel in the ancient world* (London 1979), 122); cf. rather Shaw (n. 15), 9ff.. The younger Pliny records the disappearance of his friend Atilius Scaurus on the Via Flaminia, forty miles N. of Rome; no word either, ever again, of Metilius Crispus of Comum and his party (*Epist.* 6.25).
26. Shaw (n. 15), 17f., Friedlaender, *SG* 1, 350.
27. S. Mitchell, *Journ. Rom. Stud.* 66 (1976), 106, line 24 of the Latin text (and pp. 107, 125). Cf. too Tor Hauken, *Petition and reponse* (Bergen 1998), 334ff..
28. R.W. Davies, *Service in the Roman army* (Edinburgh 1989), 66f.. Cf. too G. Wesch-Klein, *Soziale Aspetke des röm. Heerwesens* (Stuttgart 1998), 91ff. (free time), 96ff. (leave).
29. Brunt (*cit.* n. 20), 68, 396, 399, 633, 641, *id.* (1988), 253ff..
30. L. Keppie, *Making of the Roman army* (London 1984), 99f..
31. Vegetius 2.14, in chilling detail.
32. MacMullen (1963), 23ff..
33. Davies (*cit.* n. 27), 68 perhaps undervalues *le cafard*, the state of being 'browned off': cf. rather MacMullen (1963), 82f., fully confirmed by Frank Richards' extraordinary (and often reprinted by Faber, London) memoir of a private soldier's life in India, *Old soldier sahib*.
34. Davies (*cit.* n. 27), 188, 199, *Inscr. Lat. Sel.* 2238.
35. A.K. Bowman and J.D. Thomas, *Britannia* 27 (1996), 324.
36. Davies (*cit.* n. 27), 67, MacMullen (1963), 119ff..
37. MacMullen (*cit.* n. 18), J. Harmand, *L'armée et le soldat à Rome* (Paris 1967), 422ff., Y. Le Bohec, *L'armée romaine* (Paris 1989), 248; grammar: Horsfall (*cit.* n. 24 (1988)).
38. MacMullen (1963), 103f..

39. MacMullen (1990), 226ff., *id.*, (1974), 195, n. 64, L. Keppie. *Colonisation and veteran settlement* (London 1983), 110.
40. Keppie (*cit.* n. 39), 111, apparently a unique case, but startlingly in harmony with the other indications collected.
41. V. Maxfield, *Military decorations of the Roman army* (London 1981), 143.
42. Coleman (*cit.* n. 15), 415, *ead.*, *Journ. Rom. Stud.* 83 (1993), 63 *et passim*, *ead.* in Coulston-Dodge (2000), 240f..
43. Rawson (1991), 582ff..
44. Horsfall, *Mem. Amer. Acad. Rome* 41 (1996), 116; cf. p. 90ff..
45. J. Taillardat, *Les images d'Aristophane* (Paris 1962), 363ff., Usher on Thphr. *Char.* 7.4.
46. Frank (1930), 71 (e.g. *techina, machina, balista, catapulta, phylaca, machaera*), A. Otto, *Die Sprichwörter der Römer* (repr. Hildesheim 1965), 396f., Adams (1982), 158f..
47. I have read with particular pleasure and profit V. Ehrenberg, *The people of Aristophanes* (Oxford 1951), 299ff., N. Loraux, *The invention of Athens* (Eng. tr., Cambridge, Mass.), 145ff. (esp. 156), Thomas (1989), 201, 257ff., W. Rösler, in *Sympotica*, ed. O. Murray (Oxford 1990), 230ff..
48. O. Ribbeck, *Alazon* (Leipzig 1882), W. Hofmann, G. Wartenberg, *Der Bramarbas* (Berlin 1973), R. Hunter, *The new comedy of Greece and Rome* (Cambridge 1985), 66ff., N. Zagagi, *Comedy of Menander* (London 1994), 33.
49. Thomas (1992), 110.
50. Frag. 22DK. Thomas (1989), 257ff., Rösler (*cit.* n. 47), 232. Aristotle was fascinated by the evidential value of symposium-songs. Cf. my remarks at *Riv. Fil.* 122 (1994), 71.
51. Ehrenberg (*cit.* n. 47), 298, Thomas (*ib.*), 225f.. The still-unresolved confusion over the exact timing of the destruction of the Sittang Bridge during the retreat from Burma (1942) is a remarkable modern parallel.
52. Frag. 202Kock = Athen. 6.257D.
53. Thphr. *Char.* 27.3; cf. 8.4, 23.3, 25.6 (the sort of combat-stories told by cowards).
54. R.P. Saller, *Greece and Rome* 27 (1980), 69ff..
55. See e.g. Millar (*cit.* n. 21), MacMullen, as cited in nn. 16, 18, 21, 38), Corbeill (*cit.* n. 3), R. Lane Fox, *Pagans and Christians* (repr. Harmondsworth 1988).
56. As Prof. Ruurd Nauta remarks to me; cf. 10.26. Notably, *primipilares* (the senior centurion of a legion; an *eques*), 1.31.3 (with

Notes to pages 111-114

Howell's n. and 6.58.10), 93.3. At 11.3.4, though, he imagines with a shudder that his book is read by a *rigido ... centurione*! See now Nauta's *Poetry for patrons* (Leiden 2002), 71f., 133, 136.
    57. Harmand (*cit.* n. 36), MacMullen (1990), 233f.: see e.g. Suet. *Caes.* 68, Caes. *Gall.* 3.24.5, *Civ.* 3.19.1, 31.4, 48.2, 49.1, Tac. *Ann.* 1.23.3, 35.1, *Hist.* 1.18.2, 55.3, 2.27.2, 3.10.3. We shall soon see the special importance of the *carmina triumphalia*.
    58. (1993), 483.
    59. Suet. *Caes.* 58, Plut. *Caes.* 39.2, App. *Civ.* 2.61, Polyaen. 8.23.24, T. Rice Holmes, *The Roman republic* 3 (London 1923), 140.
    60. Suet. *Galba* 6.2. For marching in step to music, cf. my note on *Aeneid* 7.698 and on army song, cf. p. 111f.. See too Cupaiuolo (1993), 26ff., Some army verses were not written in the trochaic tetrameter. Thus the elegiac couplet cited at Suet. *Cal.* 8.1 was hardly for singing. Note the full discussion of the words sung to 'Colonel Bogey' in Norman Davies' *Europe* (Oxford 1996), 972f..
    61. Cf. n. 49. See further Cupaiuolo (1993), 12, Mosci Sassi (*cit.* n. 9), 43ff., Courtney (1993), 470ff., 483ff., p. 38, 65 above. Mosci Sassi's collection of army nicknames (*ib.*, 53ff.) shows that the Roman soldier had a sharp eye for his officers' build and features (Claudius, Colosseros, Cyclops, Cocles), dress (Caligula, Caracalla) and habits (Calix, Biberius Calidus Mero). Later armies likewise.
    62. Davies (*cit.* n. 27), 81ff., G.R. Watson, *The Roman soldier* (London 1969), 56, Polyb. 10.20.3, Liv. 26.51.4, 40.6.5f., Val. Max. 2.3.2, Sil. 8.548ff., Veget. 1.14, 1.15, 2.23, *Inscr. Lat. Sel.* 2487. For gladiatorial schools, see too Juv. 6.247f., Suet. *Cal.* 32.
    63. MacMullen (1990), 234, Goodyear ed. Tac. *Ann.* 1, p. 30.
    64. *Journ. Rom. Stud.* 71 (1981), 50ff. and in (ed. M. Crawford), *Sources for ancient history* (Cambridge 1983), 3-26.
    65. Cf. C. Nicolet, *Space, geography and politics in the early Roman empire* (Eng. tr., Ann Arbor 1991), T.P. Wiseman in (ed. C. Gill, TPW), *Lies and fiction* (Exeter 1993), 131. R. Syme, *Roman papers* 6 (Oxford 1991), 372ff. *et passim* is also relevant.
    66. In *Symbolae Septentrionales: Latin studies presented to Jan Öberg* (Stockholm 1995), 15ff.; thanks to Ailsa Crofts and Egil Kraggerud, I owned two copies of the paper within a fortnight of learning it existed.
    67. Davies (*cit.* n. 28), 67, Purcell (1995), 19, n. 70. Cf. p. 76.
    68. I summarised the evidence for Augustan exploration (as against conquest) in *Orazio: umanità, politica, cultura* (Perugia

1995), 23ff.. The histories of ancient geography by J.O. Thomson and E.H. Warmington may be consulted with profit.
69. Macr. *Sat.* 7.2.6 *nec non et qui obierunt maria ac terras gaudent cum de ignoto multis uel terrarum situ uel sinu maris interrogantur, libenterque respondent et describunt modo uerbis modo radio loca, gloriosum putantes, quae ipsi uiderant aliorum oculis obicere*; this depends (indirectly) on Plut. *Quaest. conv.* 2.1.
70. Handily summarised, Smith on Tib. 1.6.19f..
71. Plut. *Nicias* 12. See O.A.W. Dilke, *Greek and Roman maps* (repr. Baltimore 1998), 25f..
72. Ov. *Her.* 1.32, *Ars* 2.131f..
73. Griffin (1985).

Appendix 2

1. Full texts: E. Wistrand, *The so-called Laudatio Turiae* (Göteborg 1976) [his trans. reprinted, M.R. Lefkowitz, M.B. Fant, *Women's life in Greece and Rome*[2] (London 1992), 135ff.], D. Braund, *Augustus to Nero* (London 1985), 267-71, D. Flach, *Die sogenannte Laudatio Turiae* (Darmstadt 1991). Discussed at length, *Bull. Inst. Class. Stud.* 30 (1983), 85-98, with some updating, *Gnomon* 73 (2001), 357-9. See too S.M. Treggiari, *Roman marriage* (Oxford 1991), *passim*, R. Saller in (ed.) J.P. Bodel, *Epigraphic evidence* (London 2001), 103.
2. *Ancient society* 12 (1982), 29-31, *Bull. Inst. Class. Stud.* Suppl. 51 (1988), 53f.; cf Lefkowitz and Fant (*cit*. n. 1), 17f.. See J.A. Crook in *The family in ancient Rome* (ed. B. Rawson, London 1986), 74.
3. Cf. *Ancient history* 27 (1997), 19-23, A. Sabattini, *L'iscrizione di C. Castricio Calvo* (Bologna 1983).
4. Horsfall (1989), 199ff., Purcell (1995), 22, Rawson (1991), 570ff..
5. See Horsfall (1991), 69f..
6. After *Omnibus Omnibus* 1987, 40f.. Cf. too R. MacMullen, *Harv. Stud. Class. Phil.* 64 (1959), 215f.; K.D. White, *Greek and Roman technology* (London 1984), 160f., 215 has lost track of the sequence of events.
7. See *Zeitschr. Pap. Epigr.* 61 (1985), 251-72.

Bibliography

Adams (1982) J.N. Adams, *Latin sexual vocabulary* (London 1982)
Aldrete (1999) G.S. Aldrete, *Gestures and acclamations* (Baltimore 1999)
Arbesmann (1972) R. Arbesmann, *Die Handarbeit der Mönche* (Würzburg 1972)
Balsdon (1969) J.P.V.D. Balsdon, *Life and leisure in ancient Rome* (London 1969)
Bergmann-Kondoleon (1999) *The art of ancient spectacle*, ed. B. Bergmann, C. Kondoleon (New Haven 1999)
Bonaria (1965) M. Bonaria, *Romani mimi* (Roma 1965)
Bonner (1977) S.F. Bonner, *Education in ancient Rome* (London 1977)
Brunt (1966) P.A. Brunt, *Past and Present* 35 (1966), 3ff..
Brunt (1971) P.A. Brunt, *Social conflicts in the Roman republic* (London 1971)
Brunt (1988) P.A. Brunt, *Fall of the Roman republic* (Oxford 1988)
Cameron (1976) A. Cameron, *Circus factions* (Oxford 1976)
Chalmers (1965) W.R. Chalmers in *Roman drama*, ed. T.A. Dorey, D.R. Dudley (London 1965)
Citroni (1995) M. Citroni, *Poesia e lettori in Roma antica* (Bari 1995)
Corbett (1986) P.B. Corbett, *The scurra* (Edinburgh 1986)
Coulston-Dodge (2000) *Ancient Rome: the archaeology of the eternal city*, ed. J.C. Coulston and H. Dodge (Oxford 2000)
Courtney (1993) E. Courtney, *Fragmentary Latin poets* (Oxford 1993)
Cupaiuolo (1993) G. Cupaiuolo, *Tra poesia e politica* (Napoli 1993)
DS C. Daremberg, E. Saglio, *Dictionnaire des antiquités* (1877-1919)
Duckworth (1952) G.E. Duckworth, *Nature of Roman comedy* (Princeton 1952)

Bibliography

Dupont (1985) F. Dupont, *L'acteur-roi* (Paris 1985)
Frank (1930) T. Frank, *Life and literature in the Roman republic* (Berkeley 1930)
Friedlaender, SG L. Friedlaender, *Sittengeschichte Roms* ed. 9-10, 4 vols (Leipzig 1919-21)
Giancotti (1967) F. Giancotti, *Mimo e gnome* (Messina-Firenze 1967)
Griffin (1985) J. Griffin, *Latin poets and Roman life* (London 1985)
Gruen (1992) E. Gruen, *Culture and identity in republican Rome* (Ithaca NY 1992)
Guillemin (1937) A.-M.Guillemin, *Le public et la vie littéraire à Rome* (Paris 1937)
Habinek (1998) T.N. Habinek, *The politics of Latin literature* (Princeton 1998)
Harris (1989) W.V. Harris, *Ancient literacy* (Cambridge, Mass. 1989)
Hellegouarc'h (1963) J. Hellegouarc'h, *Le vocabulaire latin des relations et des partis politiques sous la république* (Paris 1963)
Horsfall (1987) J.N. Bremmer and NMH, *Roman myth and mythography*, Bull. Inst. Class. Stud. Suppl. 52 (1987)
Horsfall (1989) Nicholas Horsfall, *Greece and Rome* 36 (1989), 74ff., 194ff.
Horsfall (1991) Nicholas Horsfall, in *Literacy in the Roman world*, Journ. Rom. Arch. Suppl. 3 (1991), 59ff..
Horsfall (1993) Nicholas Horsfall, in *Lo spazio letterario della Grecia antica* 1.2 (ed. G. Cambiano, etc. (Roma 1993), 791ff..
Horsfall (1995), Nicholas Horsfall (ed.), *Companion to the study of Virgil* (Leiden 1995)
Horsfall (1996) Nicholas Horsfall, *La cultura della plebs romana* (Barcelona 1996)
Horsfall (1998) Rev. J.P. Small, *Wax tablets of the mind* (London 1997), Journ. Rom. Arch. 11 (1998), 565ff..
Jory (1987) E.J. Jory in *Studies in honour of T.B.L. Webster* ed. J.H. Betts, etc. (Bristol 1987), 143ff.
Jürgens (1972) H. Jürgens, *Pompa diaboli* (Stuttgart 1972)
Kaimio (1979) J. Kaimio *Romans and the Greek language* (Comm. human. Litt. 64, Helsinki 1979)
Kleberg (1957) T. Kleberg, *Hôtels, restaurants et cabarets dans l'antiquité romaine* (Uppsala 1957)
Klingshirn (1994) W. Klingshirn, *Caesarius of Arles* (Cambridge 1994)
Lane Fox (1986) R. Lane Fox, *Pagans and Christians* (London 1986)

Bibliography

Lintott (1968) A. Lintott, *Violence in republican Rome* (Oxford 1968)
MacMullen (1963)) R. MacMullen, *Soldier and civilian in the later Roman empire* (Cambridge, Mass. 1963)
MacMullen (1974) R. MacMullen, *Roman social relations* (New Haven 1974)
MacMullen (1975) R. MacMullen, *Enemies of the Roman order* (Cambridge, Mass, repr. (1975)
MacMullen (1976) R. MacMullen, *Roman government's response to crisis* (New Haven 1976)
MacMullen (1981) R. MacMullen, *Paganism in the Roman empire* (New Haven 1981)
MacMullen (1984) R. MacMullen *Christianising the Roman empire* (New Haven 1984)
MacMullen (1990) R. MacMullen, *Changes in the Roman empire* (Princeton 1990)
MacMullen (1997) R. MacMullen, *Christianity and paganism* (New Haven 1997)
Middelmann (1938) F. Middelmann, *Griechische Welt und Sprache in Plautus' Komödien* (Bochum 1938)
Millar (1977) Fergus Millar, *The Emperor in the Roman world* (London 1977)
Millar (1998) Fergus Millar, *The crowd in Rome in the late republic* (Ann Arbor 1998)
Millar (2002) Fergus Millar, *Rome, the Greek world and the East* 1 (Chapel Hill 2002)
Mouritsen (2001) H. Mouritsen, *Plebs and politics in the late Roman republic* (Cambridge 2001)
MRR T.R.S. Broughton, *Magistrates of the Roman republic* (2 vols, New York 1951, 1952)
Nicolet (1976) C. Nicolet, *Le métier du citoyen* (Paris 1976)
Nippel (1995) W. Nippel, *Public order in ancient Rome* (Cambridge 1995)
Noy (2000) D. Noy, *Foreigners at Rome* (London 2000)
Opelt (1965) I. Opelt, *Die lateinischen Schimpfwörter* (Heidelberg 1965)
Otto (1965) A. Otto, *Die Sprichwörter der Römer* (repr. Hildesheim 1965)
Purcell (1994) Nicholas Purcell, *Cambridge Ancient History* 9^2 (Cambridge 1994), 644ff.
Purcell (1995) Nicholas Purcell, *Past and Present* 147 (1995), 3ff.

Bibliography

PW Pauly-Wissowa, *Realencyclopädie der classischen Altertumswissenschaft* (Stuttgart 1893-)
Ramage (1973) E.S. Ramage, *Urbanitas* (Norman, Oklahoma 1973)
Rawson (1985), E. Rawson, *Intellectual life in the late Roman republic* (London 1985)
Rawson (1991) E. Rawson, *Roman culture and society* (Oxford 1991)
Scobie (1983) A. Scobie, *Apuleius and folklore* (London 1983)
Seager (1969) *Crisis of the Roman republic*, ed. R. Seager (Cambridge 1969)
Taylor (1964) L.R. Taylor, *Party politics in the age of Caesar* (Berkeley 1964)
Thomas (1989) Rosalind Thomas, *Oral tradition and written record* (Cambridge 1989)
Thomas (1992) Rosalind Thomas, *Literacy and orality* (Cambridge 1992)
Tosi (1991) R. Tosi, *Dizionario delle sentenze latine e greche* (Milano 1991)
Väterlein (1976) J. Väterlein, *Roma Ludens* (Amsterdam 1976)
Vanderbroeck (1987) P.J.J. Vanderbroeck, *Popular leadership ...* (Amsterdam 1987)
Weismann (1972) W. Weismann, *Kirche und Schauspiele* (Würzburg 1972)
Wiedemann (1992) T. Wiedemann, *Emperors and gladiators* (London 1992)
Wille (1967) G. Wille, *Musica Romana* (Amsterdam 1967)
Wiseman (1985) T.P. Wiseman, *Catullus and his world* (Oxford 1985)
Wiseman (1987) T.P. Wiseman, *Roman studies* (Liverpool 1987)
Wiseman (1994) T.P. Wiseman, *Historiography and imagination* (Exeter 1994)
Wiseman (1998) T.P. Wiseman, *Roman drama and Roman history* (Exeter 1998)
Wright (1931) F.W. Wright, *Cicero and the theater* (Northampton, Mass., 1931)
Yavetz (1988) Z. Yavetz, *Plebs and princeps* (2nd ed., New Brunswick 1988)

Index

accent 26f.
accentual verse, beginnings of 127
acclamations 24
accountancy 12
acroama (dinner-entertainment) 71
actors, travelling 55, 72
Alexandria, populace of 28f.
Allia Potestas 126ff.
allusions and public 41
anecdote, and history 89f., military 111, and taverns 107, and travel 114
Anna Perenna, festival of 12f.
appearance of soldier 104
applause, and seating 41, ill-timed 40, purchased 38ff., rhythmic 40, signalled 40, types of 40
arena, changes in 23f.
aretalogus 57
aristocracy and music 31ff., 35
army, and gladiators 112, and Greek 49, 51, and social mobility 111, and travel 114, closed society 106f., gambled 77, stories 113, tedium and drink 107, transfers within 106
art, and education 159, n. 54, and history 90f.
Athens, demos of 28f.
audibility 87
audience, flattered 84, of historical art 91, sabotage by 61ff., theatre mixed 58
Augustine, St 42
Augustus, and entertainments 68, 70f., and musicians 34, companions of 70f., tastes of 78, 100
authorship of popular 'literature' 64

backgammon 76f.
ball-games 76
banditry 106
banquet, dramatic 69f.
banqueting songs 33, 96, 97f.
barracking 87
baths, emperor visits 112
battles, re-enacted 109, veterans of individual 108
bears 61f.
bedtime songs 43
beer in army 107
beggars' chants 44
betting 153, n. 16
bogeymen 81
booty and history 91f.
boxers 62
bread, see circuses
buffoon 70f.
busker, see *circulator*

Caesar and elks 113

Index

Caesarius of Arles 14f.
calculations, duodecimal 18f.
canabae 107
carmina convivalia 33, 96, 97f.
carmina triumphalia 111f.
Castricius, C. 122ff.
Cena Trimalchionis 52
centurions 104, 110, 113
change in popular entertainments 23f.
charlock, white 111
Christian attacks on popular entertainment 24
Christianity, and dance 17, and memorisation 14f., and work song 15f.
Cicero 83ff., blinkered 69f., inconsistent on *plebs* 84, insults *plebs* 86, 93f., language of contempt 93f., on art 83, on theatre, 83f., snobbery of 75
circulator (busker) 57, 79, 98f.
circus, bread and 28ff., changes in 23
civilians and soldiers 105f.
claque 39
class-mixing 77
collegia, entertainments of 33, 72, meetings of 56
Columella on *plebs* 29f.
comedy, decline of 59f., revivals of 58
common fund 100, entertainments and 77f.
conservatism 123
contio 87, cross-examination at 88
control of popular culture 38ff.
conversation and entertainments 75
corn dole at Alexandria 28f.
country, intellectual tastes 85
countryside, conservatism in 122f.
courts, reactions in 39
cricket, and Romans 100f.

cries, vendors' 43
criminals and soldiers 105
criticisms, misleading 36
cross-class dinners 77, friendships 100
cultural hierarchy 66

dance 34ff., and Christians 17, 35, and morals 35
dance-school 35
detail, vulgarity of 21f., why present in texts 21ff.
dicing 76f.
die is cast 155, n. 41
diet, army 111
dinner-entertainment 71
dirty stories 79
Douglas, Kirk 112
dress 26f.
drill, parodied 112
duodecimal system 12, 17f.

education, and rank 27, by art 159, n. 54
elks 113
emperor, and music 34, and veterans 112, naked 68, tastes of 70
engineers, military 124ff.
Ennius, public readings 56
entertainments and daily talk 75
epitaphs 64, indelicate 128, signed, 64
Etruscan, plays in 53
exempla 90, Cicero's 94f.
exile, returns from 89
expertise, compromising 32

fables 81f.
factions, circus 40
farming 122f.
flattery of audience 84
fractions 12, 18f.

Index

freedmen in Petronius 71
funeral orations 119

gamblers, distinguished 77
games, children's 46
gaming 30, 76f., in army 114
generalisations, ancient 26
geography 87
Georgics 69
ghost stories 78f.
gladiators 62, and army 112, enthusiasm for 76
goats and music 33
graffiti 64
Greek immigrants 50, and luxury 51, and music 32, jobs of 51
Greek, and army 49, and business 49f., and commerce 51f., and farming 51, at Pompeii 52, dialects of 68, in theatre 49, 53, plays in 53

Hadrian 112
handicaps, physical 104
hats 22
heresy 42
hexameters 127
hierarchy of Roman culture 66
historical knowledge of audience 89
historical tragedy 90, 97, 160, n. 3
history, and booty 91f., and *contio* 88ff., and proverbs 91, and storyelling 80, learning of 87, popular appeal of 84f.
Homer and popular culture 55
Huizinga, J. 153, n. 12
hymns 24, and doctrine 42

illiterates and memory 17
immigrants, cluster 50
improvised poetry, fashionable 55f.
inheritances 18

inscriptions 116ff.
inscriptions and reading 92
insula, educational 50
insults, inherited, 28ff., launched 41f., super-adhesive 42
interest 18f.

jingles 11
joke-books 70

knights, wealth of 27

Lamiae 81
language, military 49,104, 107, 109, 113
latrines and poetry 55
Laudatio Murdiae 119ff.
Laudatio Turiae (*sic*) 116ff.
leave in army 106f.
levels and farming manuals 68
levels, cultural 68f.
life, daily, not observed 21ff.
literacy 30, 66, 72ff., alternatives to 48ff., 65, and political life 74
loans 18
lovers' songs 44
ludi, how frequent 13
luxury and Greeks 51

Maecenas, and music 34, tastes of 70f., 78
manipulation of reactions 38ff.
manuals, farming 68f.
maps drawn in wine 114f.
maxims 123f.
medals 108
memories of soldiers 109ff.
memories of war 105f.
memorisation 11ff., and Christianity 14f., and reading 15, and song 11ff., aversion to 15, Christian, failure of 15ff., no decline in 14, selective 15

Index

memory, and army-song 112, and literacy 17, and popular culture 72f., and song 24f.
metre, popular 38
metrical sense of *plebs* 85f.
metrical unity 65
miles gloriosus 109f.
Milesian tales 80
military language 49
military service, educational 48f.
mime 60, 128, and philosophy 54f., sex in 80
money, see wealth
monks, and memorisation 14f., and music 15f.
moral level in theatre 60
music, and Rome 25, 31ff., and status 31f., and Trimalchio 32f., 35, music universal at Rome 33
musical skill, prejudice against 31f., skills recorded 33f.
musicians, hired 34
mutinies 111, 113
myth, transmission of 98f.
mythology, and pantomime 60, in theatre 58

names on works of art 91
Naples 52
neighbourhood and status 26
nicknames 113
noble hooligans 77
Nonius Datus 124ff.
nudity and status 68
nurses 81, songs of 43

obscenity 79
observation, disinclination of Romans 21
oligarchic insults 29
oral history 96
oral sources, citation of 97
orality and Rome 25f.

orator, and *contio* 87, and popular audience 86
Oscan, plays in 53
Ostia, theatre at 57
ovationes 92
Ovid, narrative detail in 20f., performed 56

pantomime 59f., version of poetry in 56
parasitus 70
parody of drill 112
pattern-books 64
percentages 12
performances, repeat 13
Petronius, Greek in 52, humour of 71, world of 32f., 35, 52
philosopher, wandering 54, in mime 54f., widespread traces of 55
physiological theory 103f.
pigs, musical 33
pleasure taken in theatre 136, n. 53
plebs, and allusions 13f., and Greek 49, and history 84f., and philosophy 84, and political activity 99f., and theatre 13, characterised by Cicero 86, 93f., definition of 26ff., differences within 27, ear of 85f., knowledge of plays 13f., insults against 28ff., reading tastes 85, role in politics 66, terminology for 26f.
Pliny the Younger, tastes 78f.
poetry in theatre 56
poets, epitaphs of 64, wandering 55
political activity of *plebs* 99f., and literacy 74
political involvement 27, 66, 87
Pompeii, Greek at 52
popular audience and orator 86

Index

popular culture, boom in 54, decried 65f., durable 35f.
popular reactions, manipulated 38ff.
populus, see *plebs*
pornography 79f.
prejudice, Roman 83, Roman, ineffectual 32, 35
privations, in army 111
professional skill eschewed 32
programmes, mixed 57
protest, organisation of 41f.
proverbs 65, 69, 81,123f., and history 91
public and allusions 41
public documents, read 73f.
public life, activity in 87
public men, cross-examined 88, simple tastes of 78

rank and education 27
reaction, popular, for sale 38ff.
readers of public documents 73f.
reading and memorisation 15
ready reckoners 12
re-enactments of battles 109
religious texts memorised 14
revivals in theatre 13
rhythm 37f., flawed sense of 121, *plebs*' sense of 85f.
riddles 47, 65, 81
Rome, and music 25, and orality 25, as museum 91
routine, army 107
rowers' songs 15, 44
rustics' intellectual tastes 85

sabotage, theatre, aim of 61ff.
sailors' songs 44
Sallust and Sempronia 31f.
scars 104
scurra 70

seating, and reaction 41, organisation of 41
Sempronia and music 31f.
sententia 60
shepherds' songs 44
sieges 111
slave household, educational 50
snobbery and wealth 27
social historian's sources 20ff.
social memory 61, 65, 88
soldiers, and civilians 105f., and criminals 105, appearance of 103, in Italy/Rome 106, maimed 104, memories of 109ff., retire together 107f.
soldiers, playing at 46
soldiers' Greek 49, Latin 104, 107, 109, 113, songs 43
song 36f., and memory 24f., army 112, at work 36, authorship of 38, contemporary reference in 23, diffusion of 37, fragments of 45ff., in context 43ff., insulting 37, memorised 12f., respectable 33,36, work-songs and Christians 15f.
sources and social history 20ff.
stage of public life 88
Statius, performed 56f.
stories in army 113
storytelling 78f., and history 80
street-vendors 43
style, military 126
stylistic weaknesses 119
Suetonius and physiology 103
symposium-songs 98

table, songs at 43
tables, memorised 11f.
Tacitus, soldiers in 110
tall tales 80, and history 113, soldiers' 113
tastes, simple of public figures 78

Index

tavern music 15, 31
taverns, and anecdote 107, and memorisation 15, and morals, 107, and music 31, 35, frequented by wealthy 77
taverns, maps drawn in 114f.
Terence, criticisms of 62f.
theatre, allusions in 41, and memorisation 12f., 15f., and pleasure 136, n. 53, and poetry 56, choice of plays 59, disorder in 41, divisions in 67, ducative 54, history of 59, how often visited 13, love for 59, polyglot 53, programmes 57, revivals in 13, sabotage in 61ff., seriousness in 60, special effects 59, theatre culture, static 23, unity of audience 67f.
theatre-song, and work 16, wins Christians 16
Tiberius 70
tightrope-walkers 62
Titus, emperor 85
toga 26f.
traders in Greek world 49f.
tragedies, old, love for 59
tragedy, decline of 59f., historical 90, 97, 160, n. 3
travel and anecdote 114
travellers' songs 44
Trimalchio, and music 32f.. 35, cultural play 71, tastes 76
triumphal processions 91, 109

triumphs 92
triumph-songs 38, 65, 111f.
trochaic tetrameter 38

underwear 22
uniform, legionary 103
unity, metrical 38
urban life, elusive detail of 22
Ustinov, Peter 112

Varro 68f.
veterans, and emperor 112, and Greek 49, privileges of 108, status of 106, togetherness of 107f.
Virgil, memorised 11, 15, performed 56
vocabulary, repetitious 119, 121f.
voice, trained 88
Volteius Mena 67, 69, 100

wealth and esteem 27
weapons training 112
wedding-songs 43
weights and measures 17f.
werewolves 80
wine in army 107
winter quarters 107
Wiseman, T.P. 160, n. 2
work-songs 36, 45, and theatre songs 16

xenophobia 51

www.ingramcontent.com/pod-product-compliance
Lightning Source LLC
Chambersburg PA
CBHW051101230426
43667CB00013B/2395